RARA
ANIMALIA
UNI-RELIC
CODEX

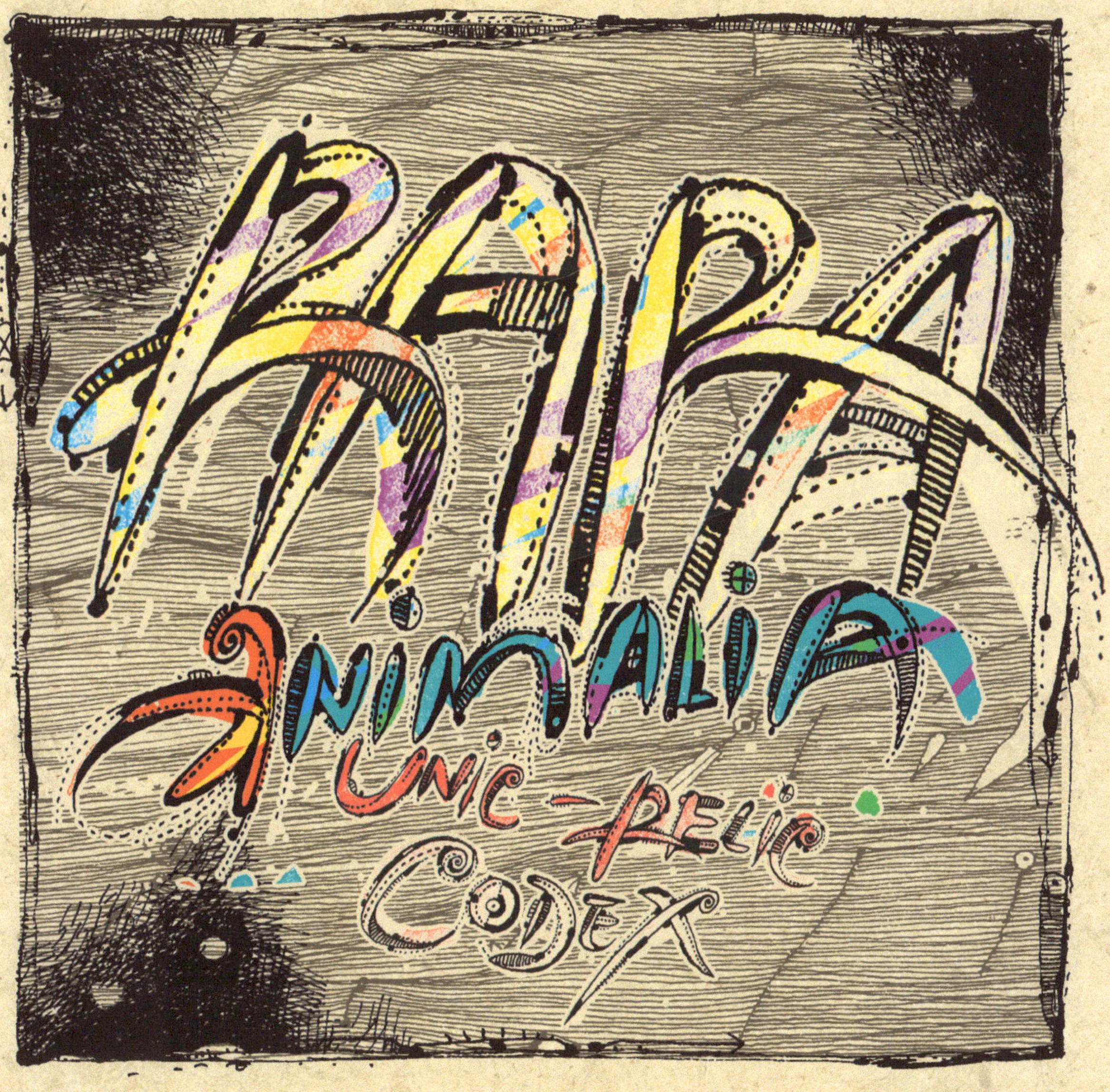

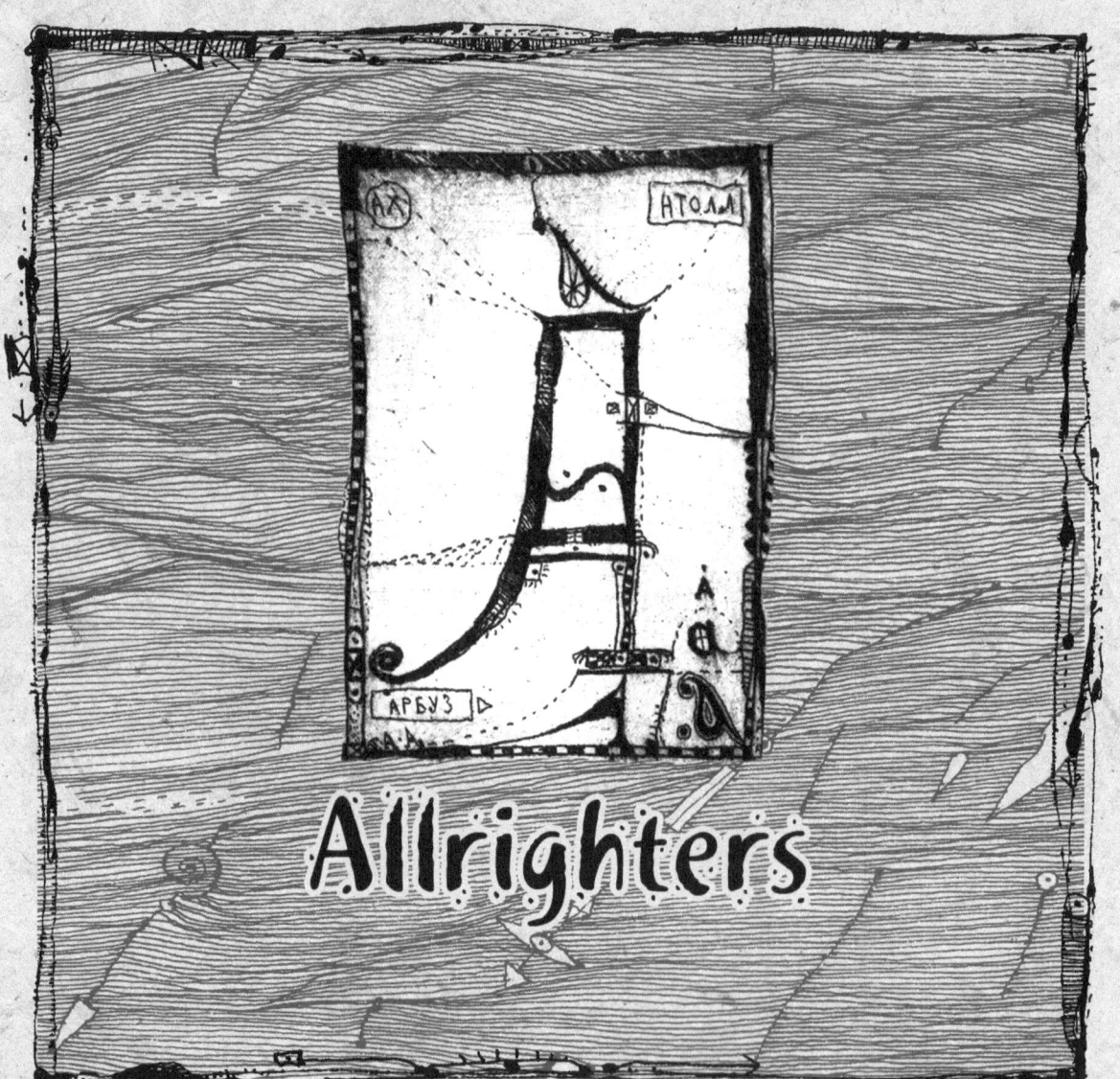

Allrighters

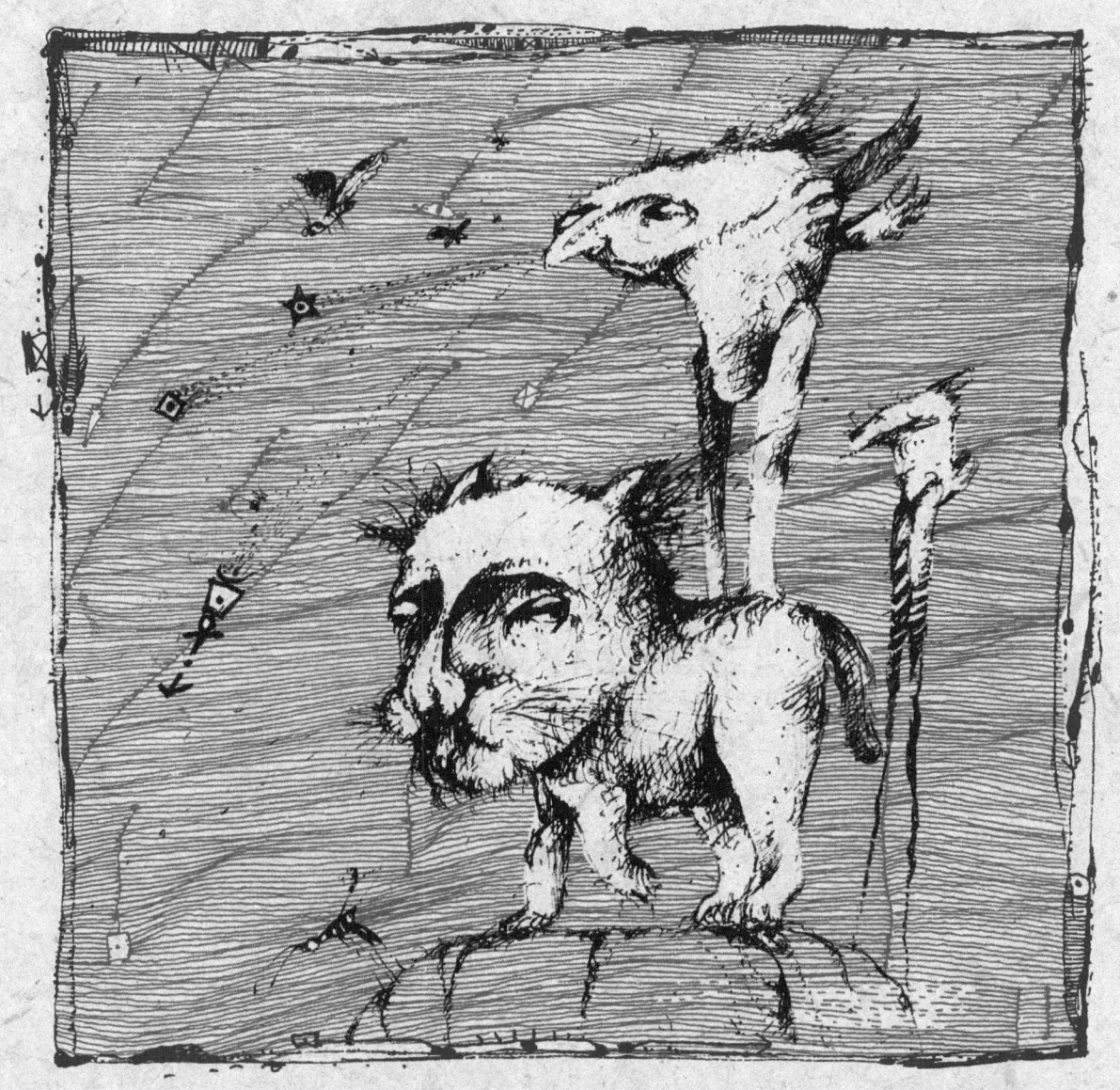

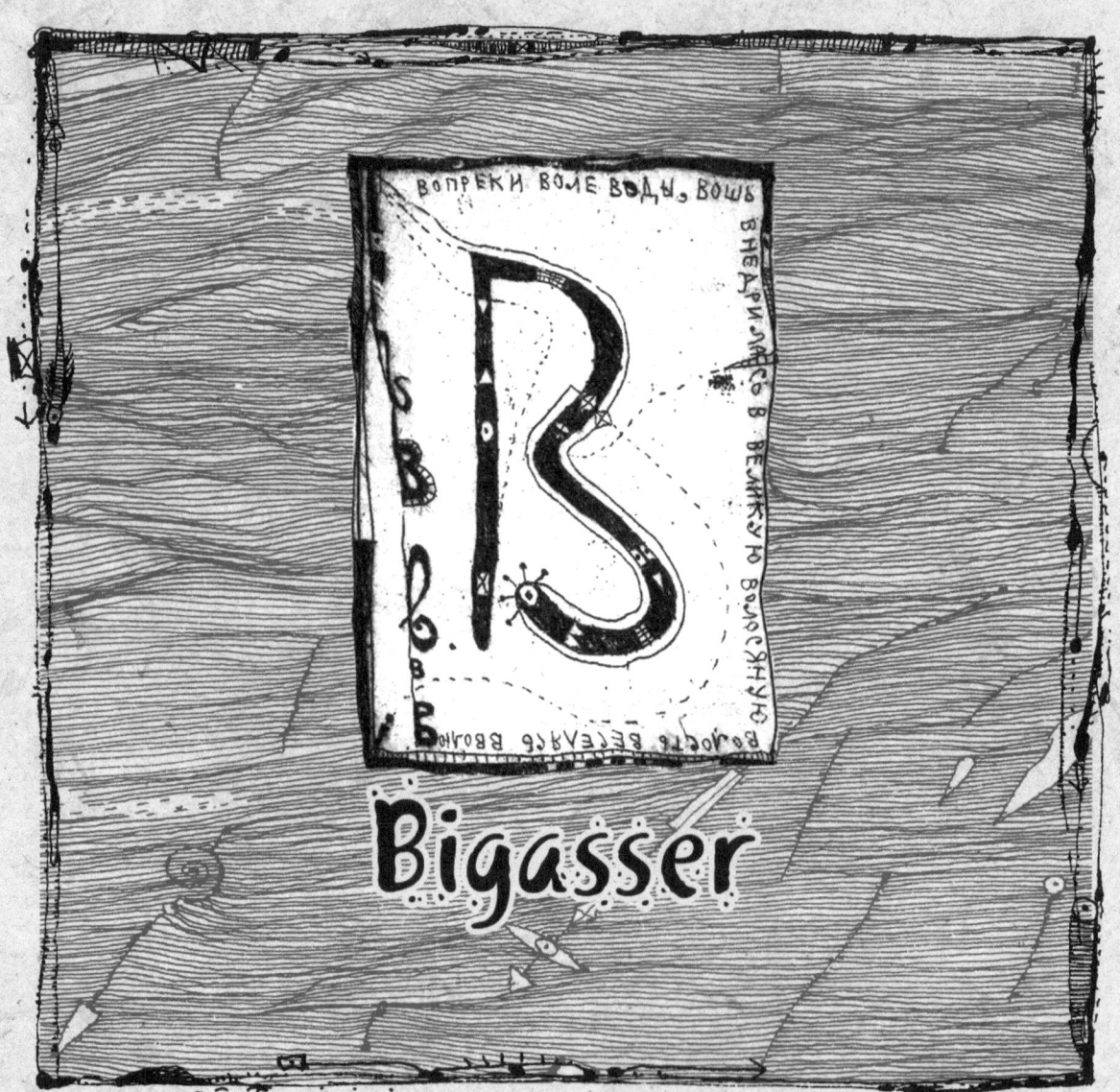

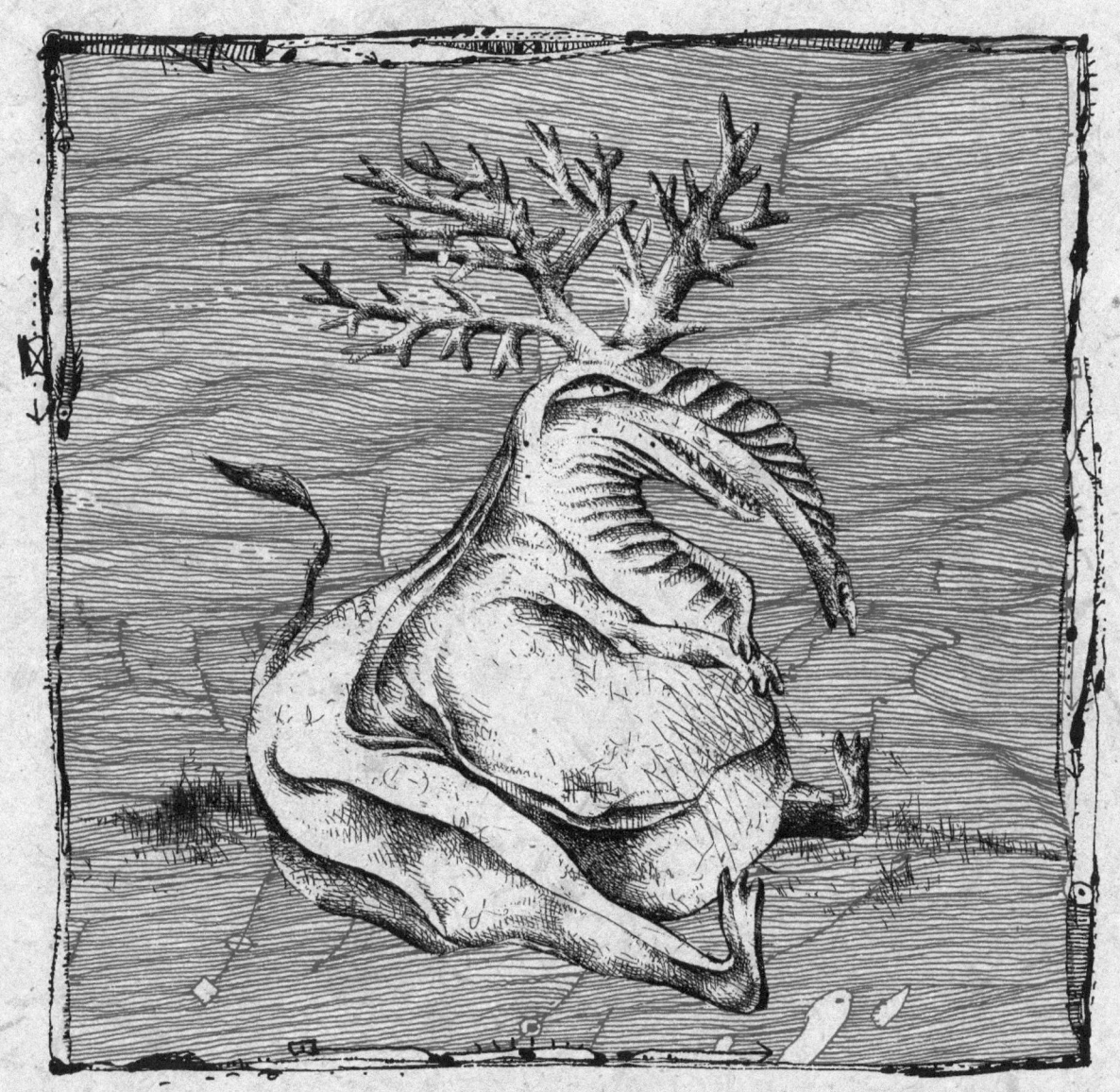

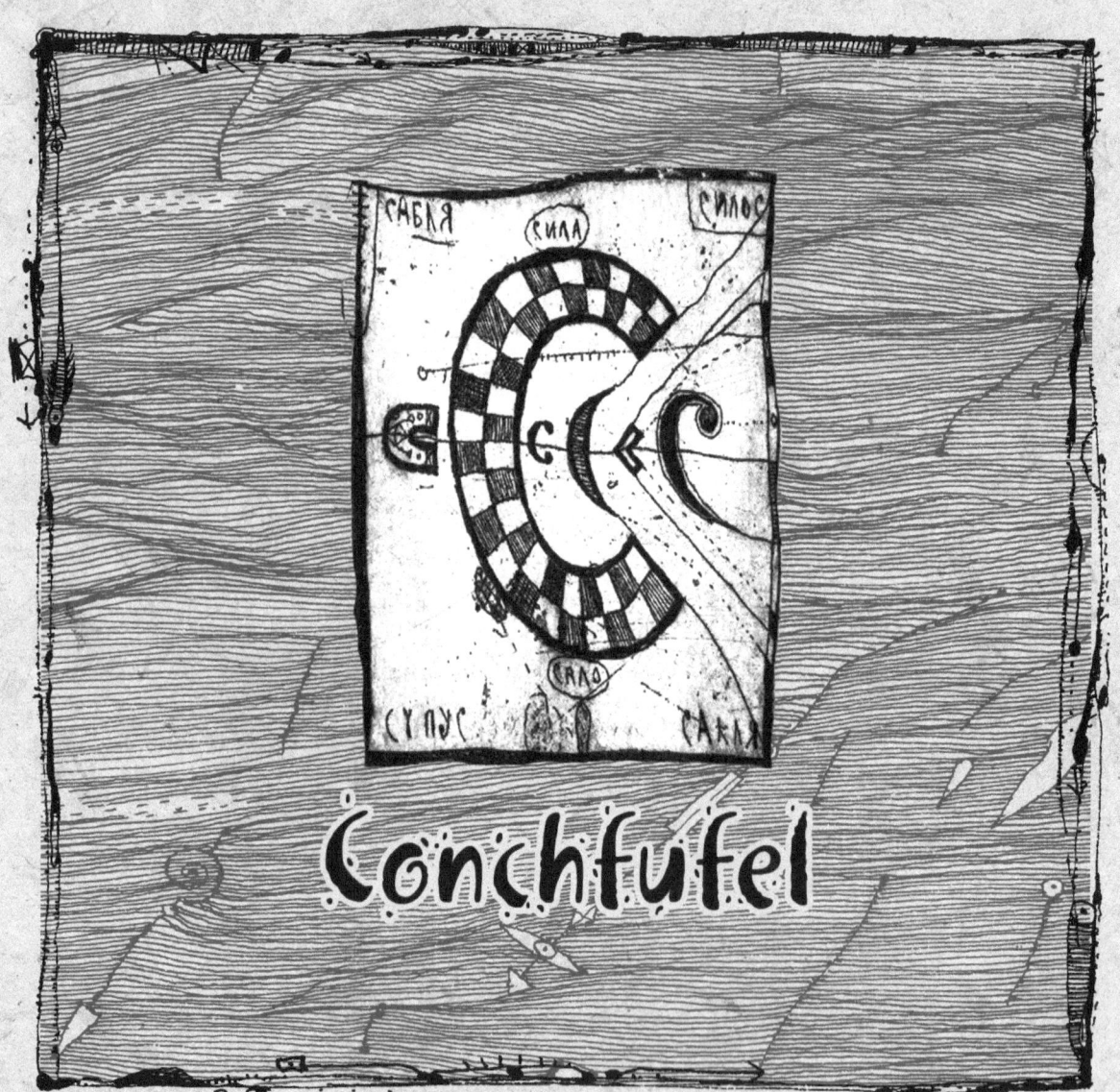

Conchtufel

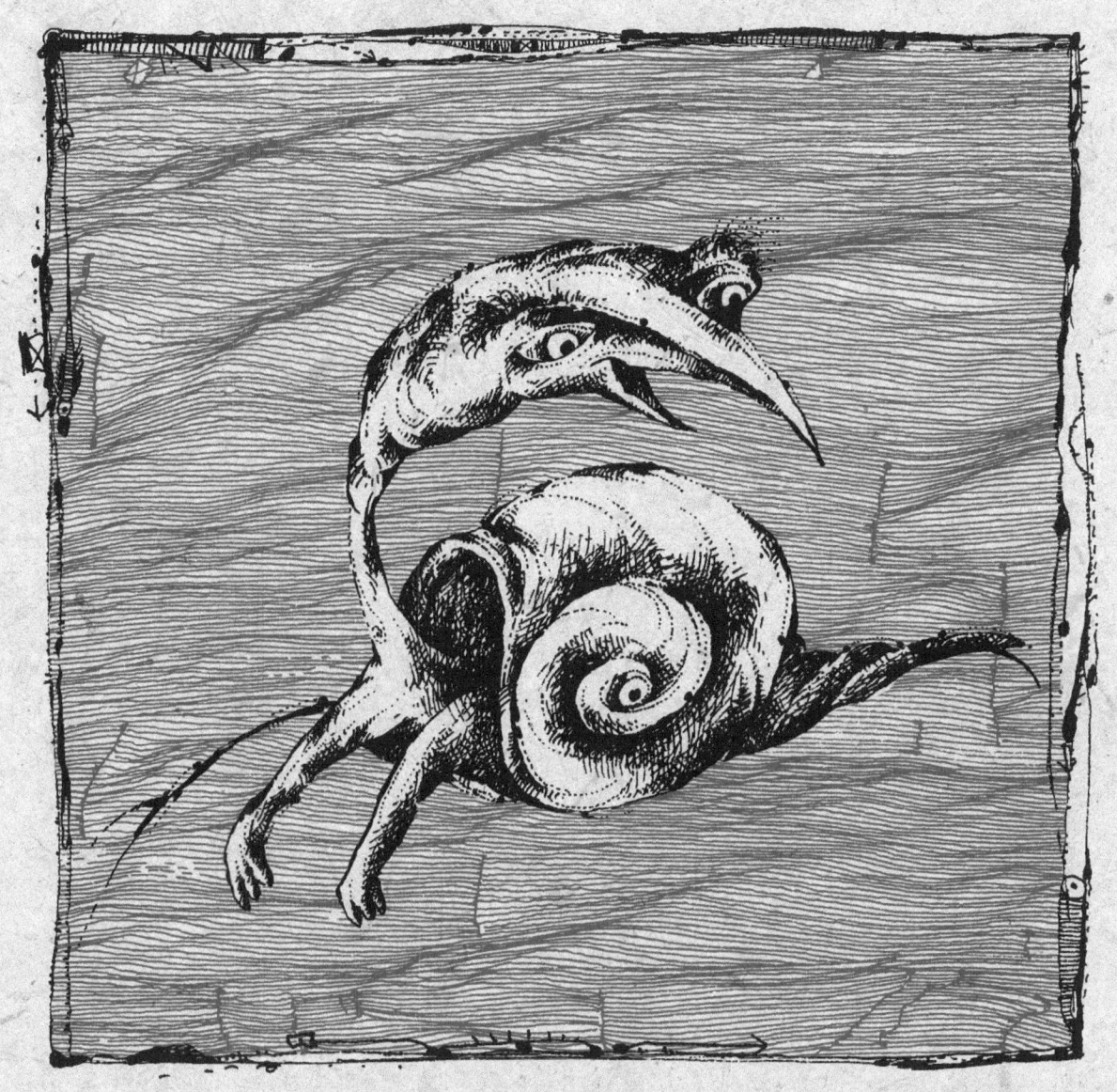

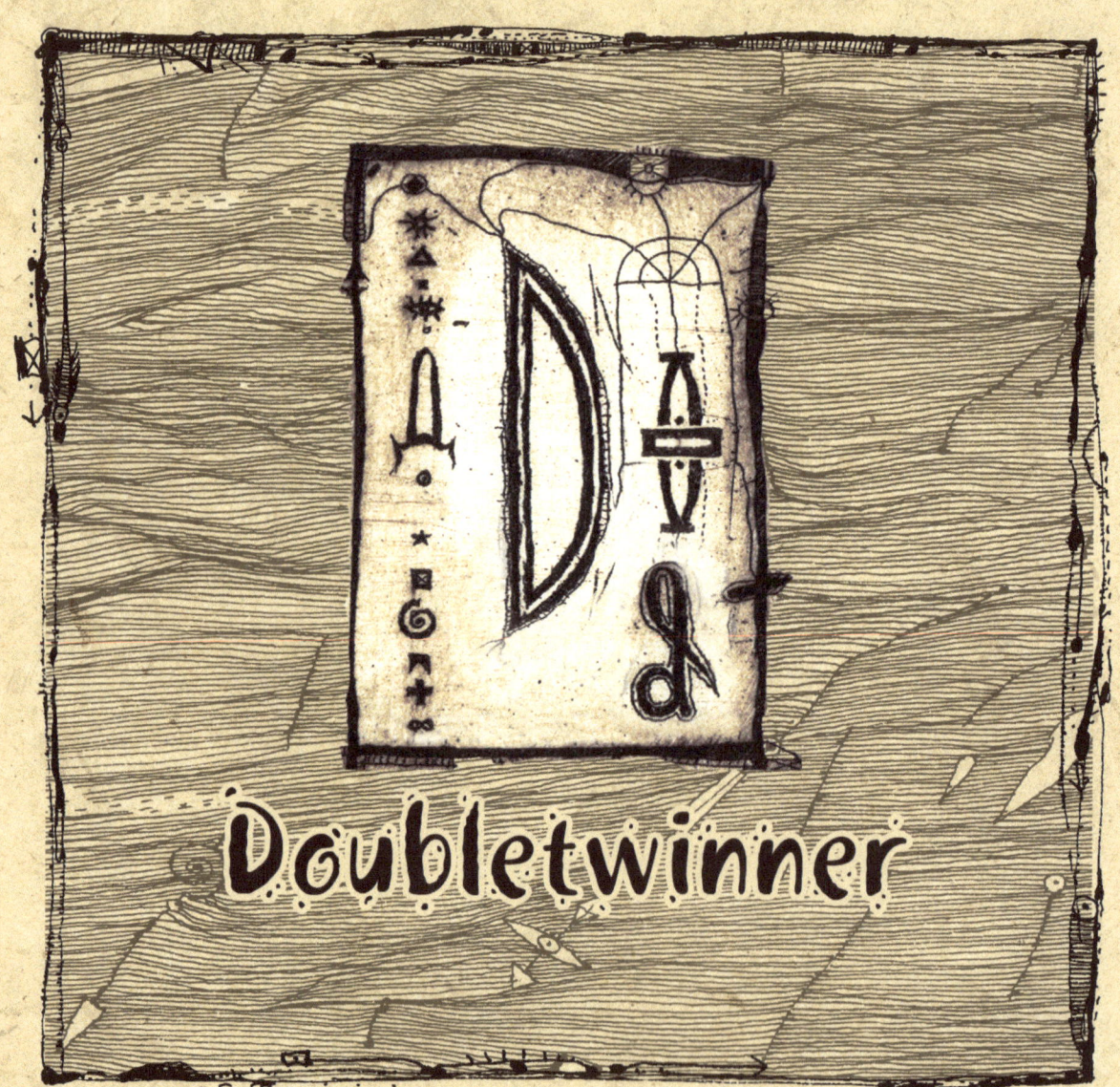

Doubletwinner

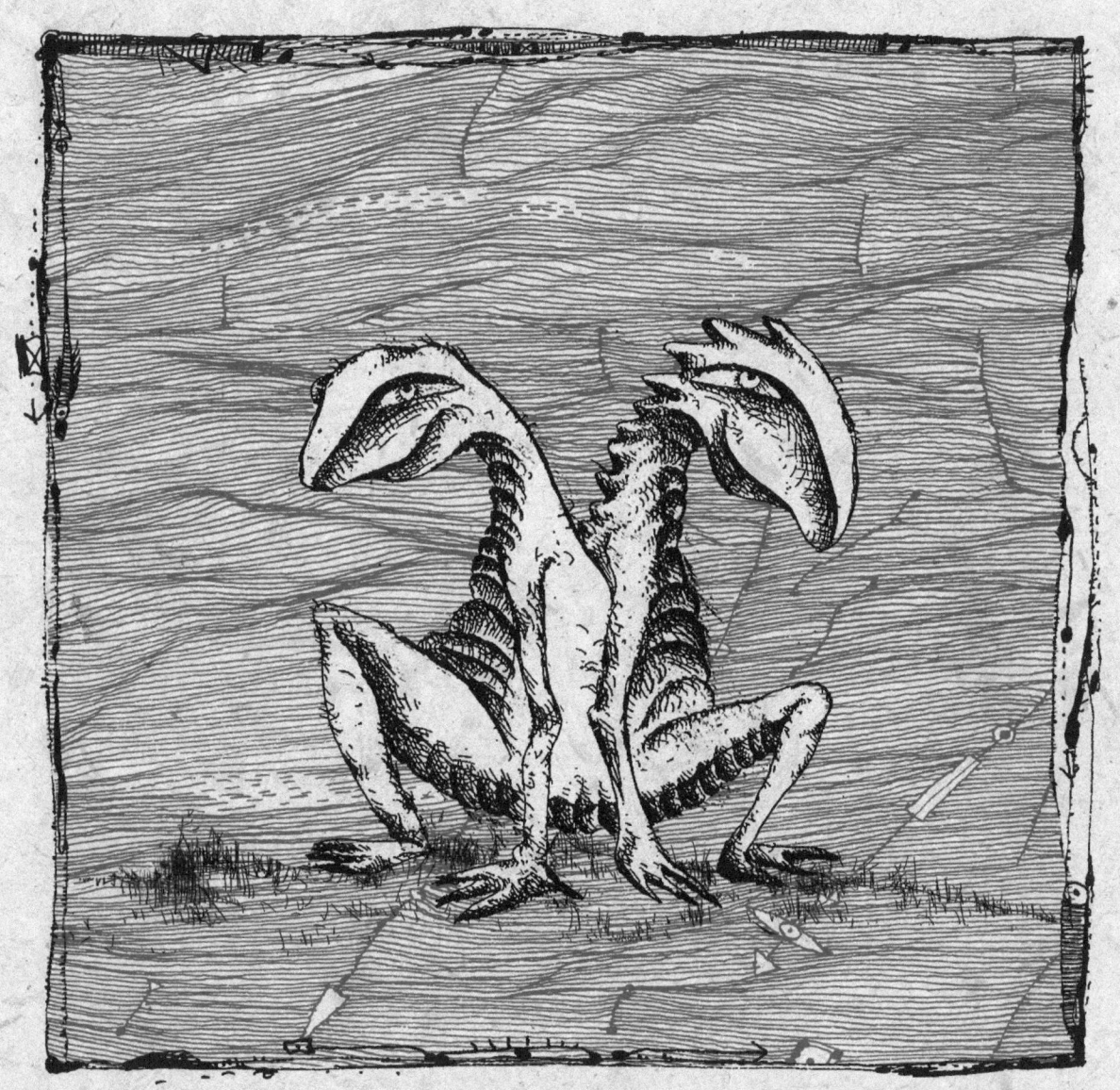

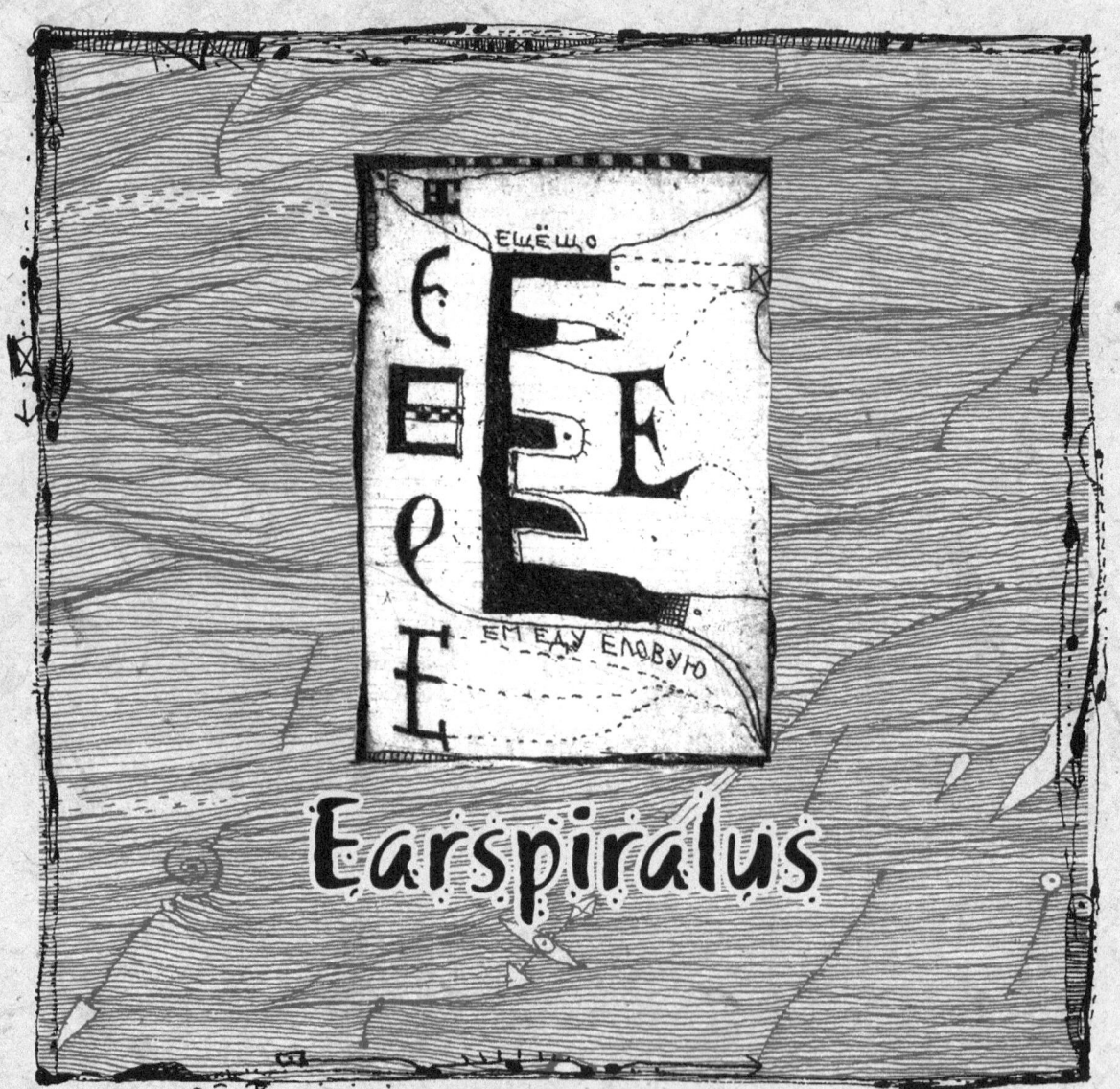

Earspiralus

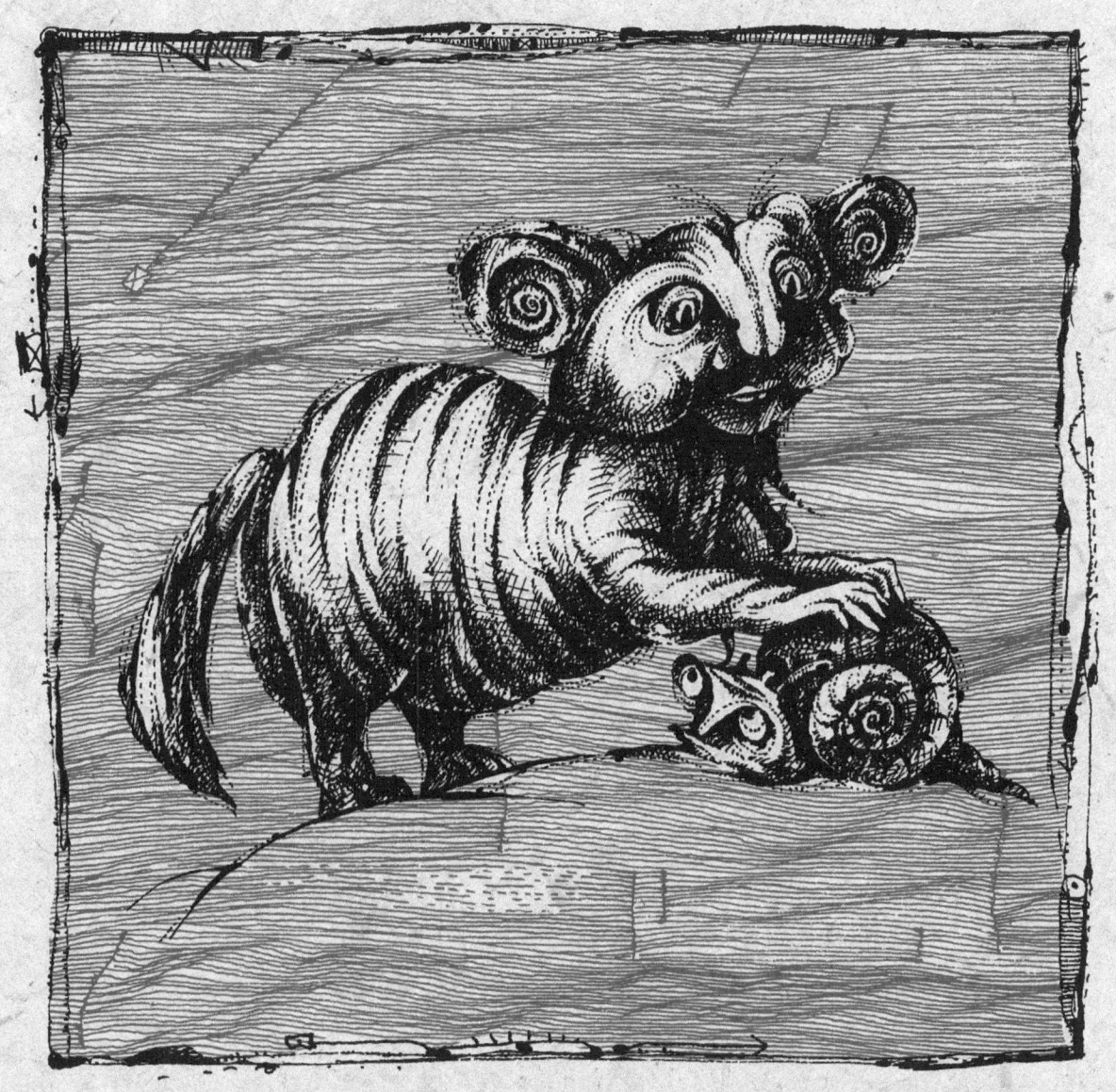

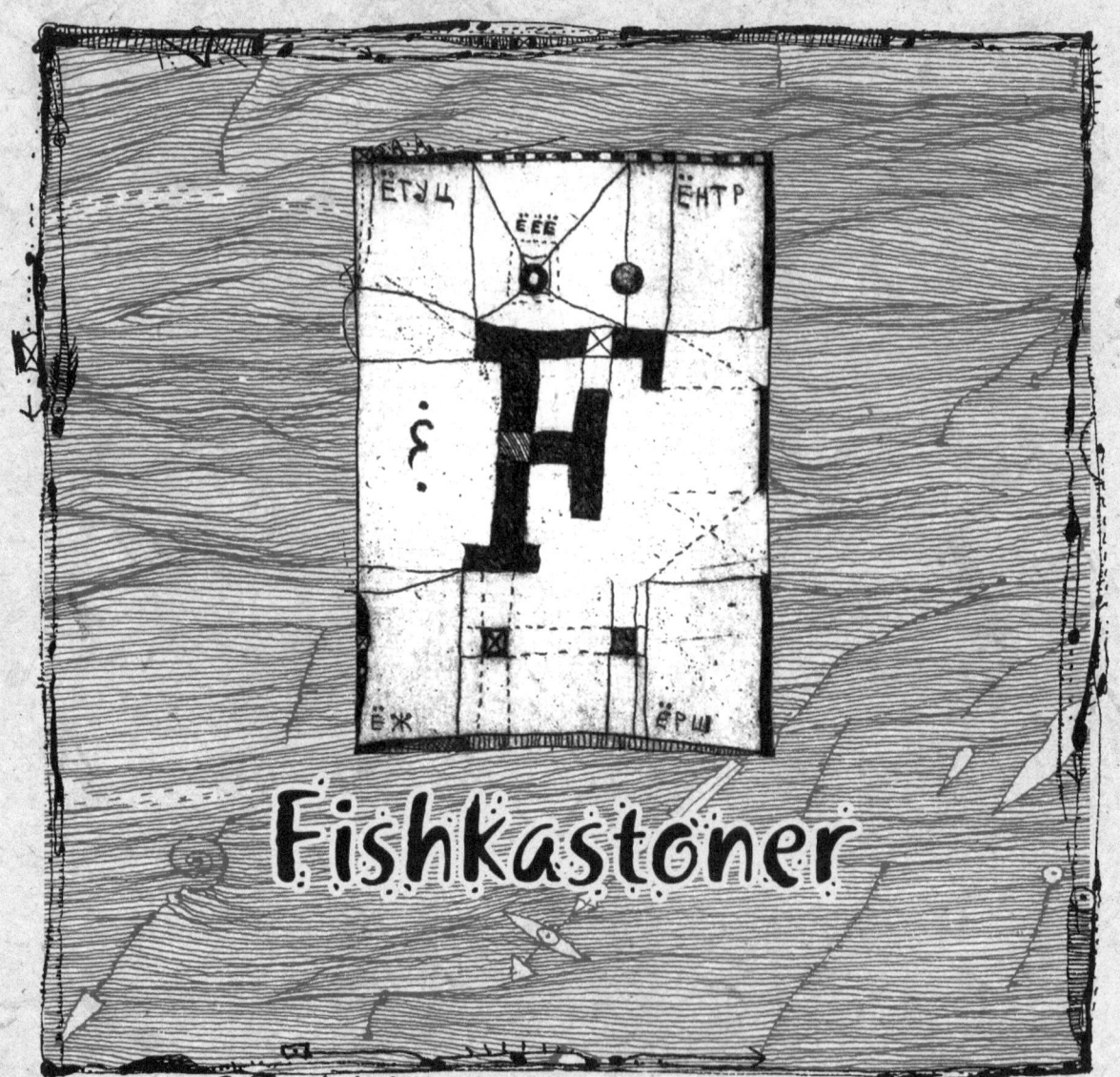

Fishkastoner

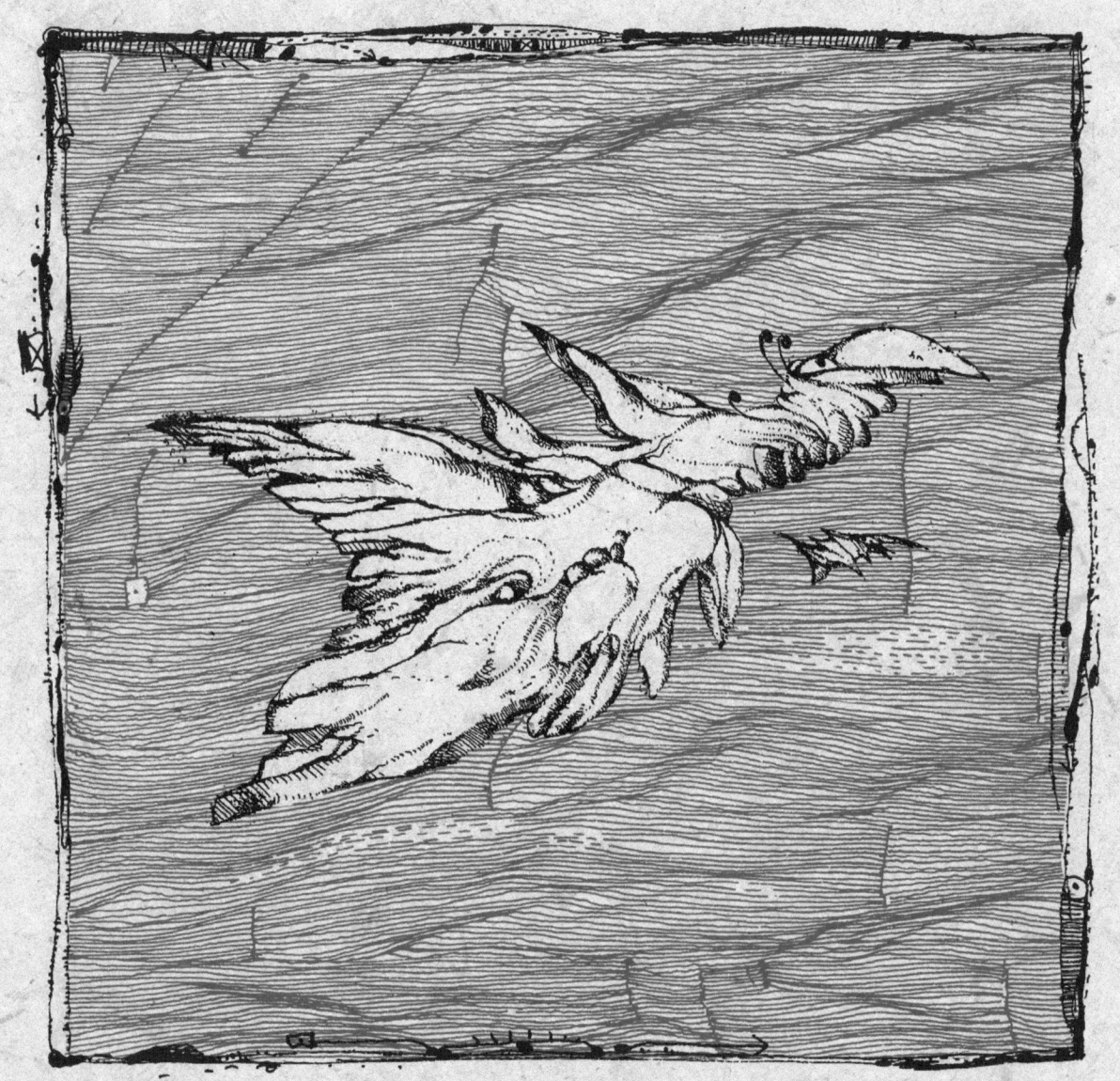

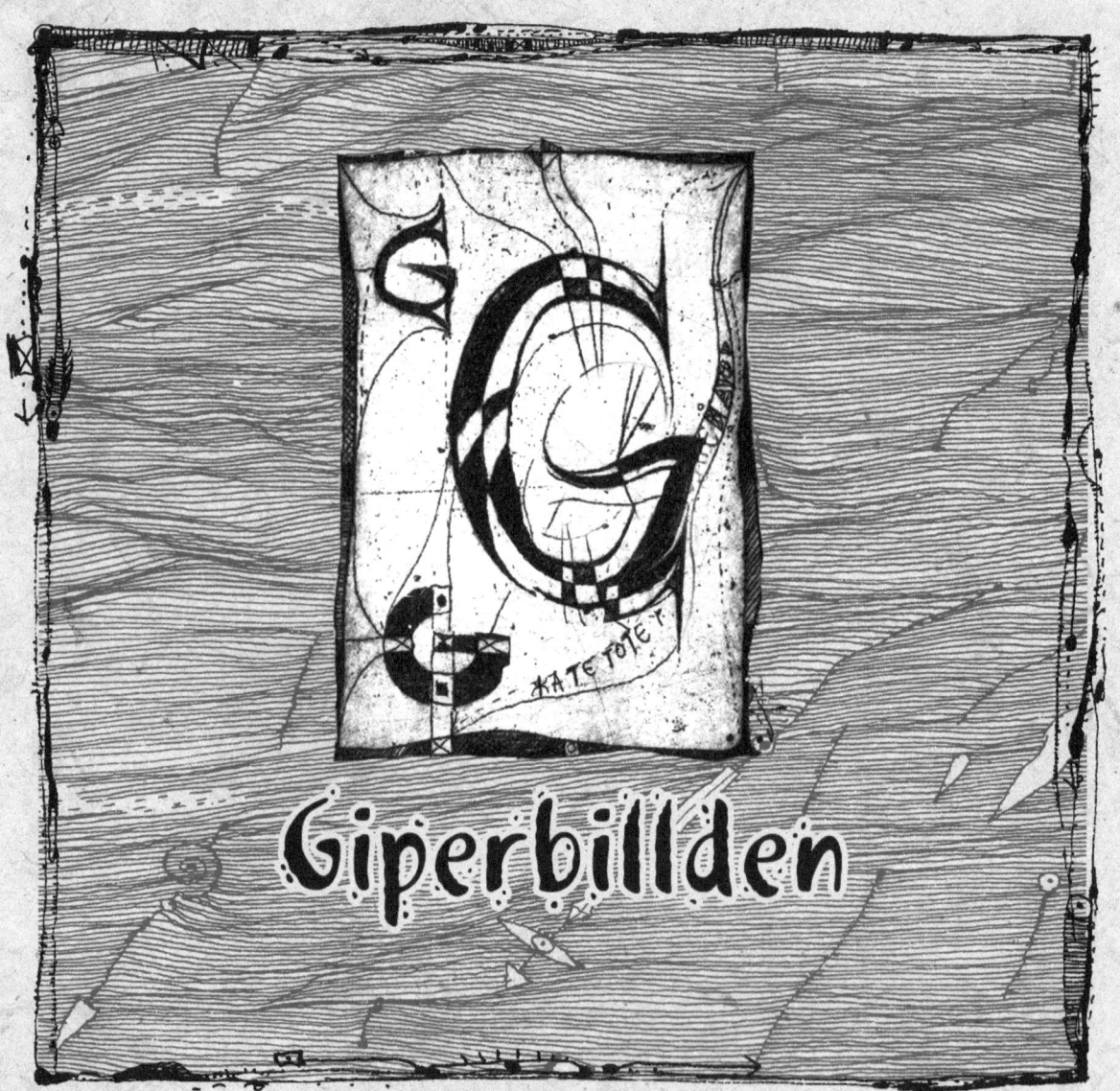

Giperbillden

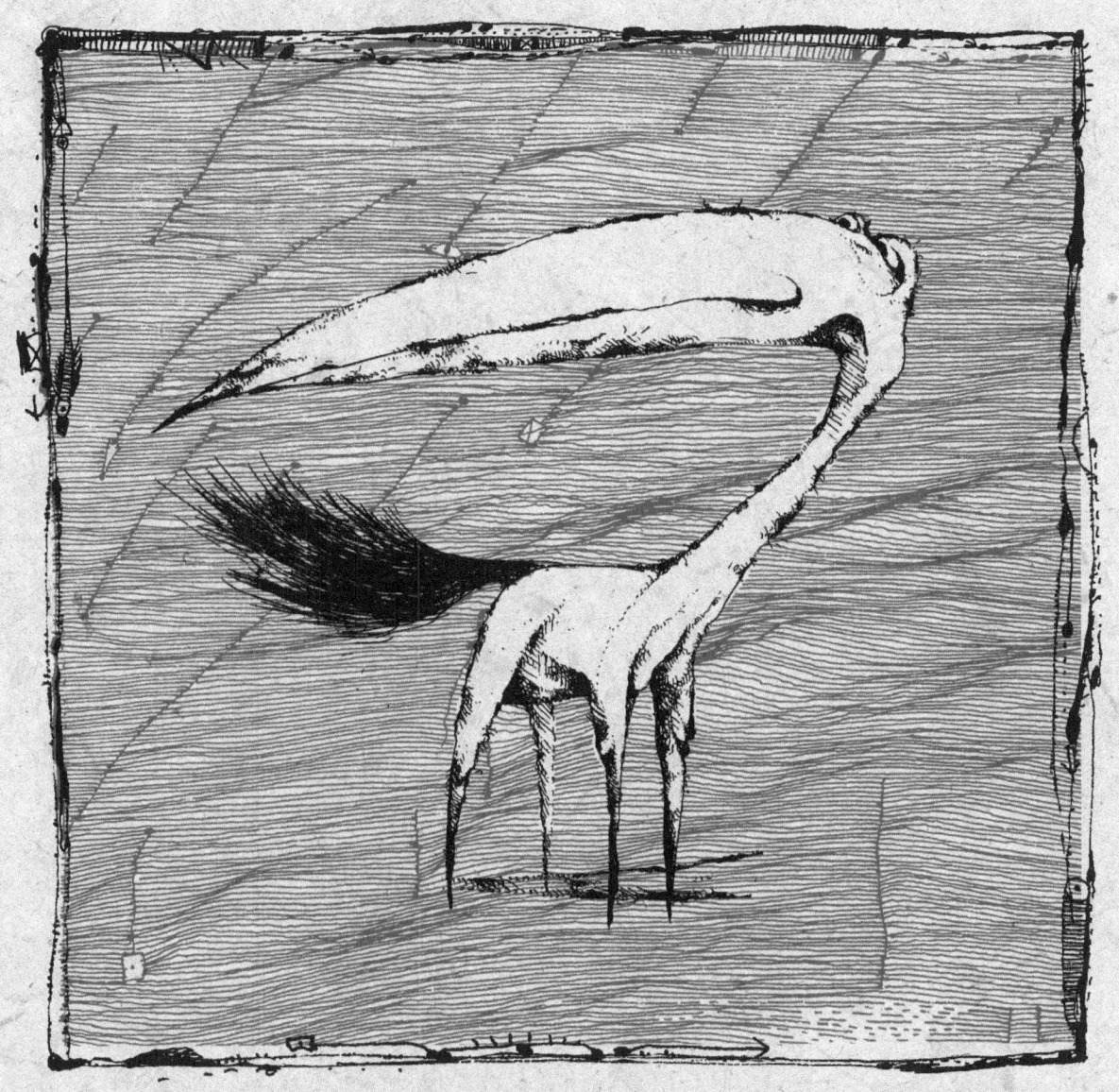

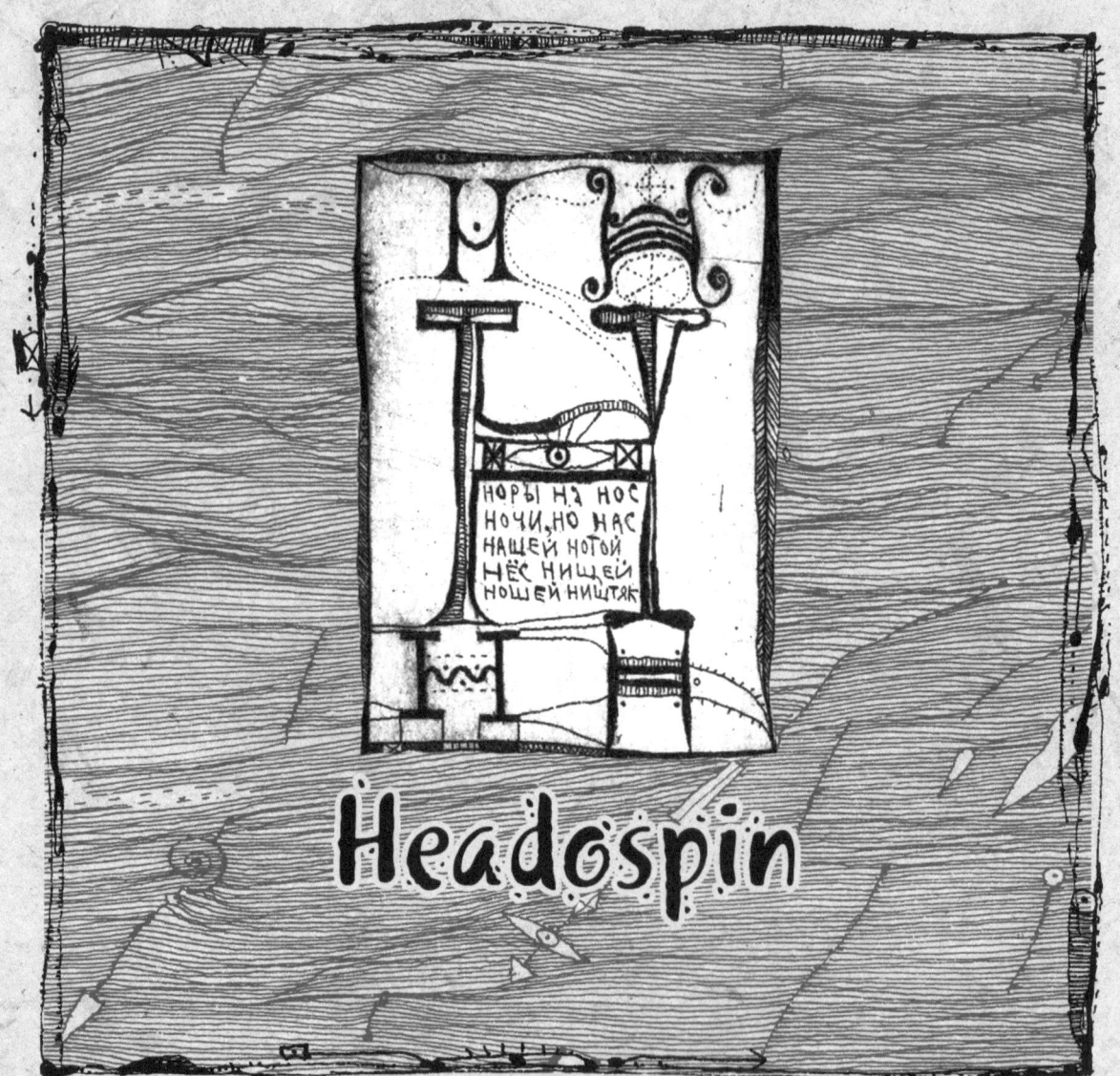

НОРЫ НА НОС
НОЧИ, НО НАС
НАШЕЙ НОТОЙ
НЁС НИЩЕЙ
НОШЕЙ НИШТЯК

Headospin

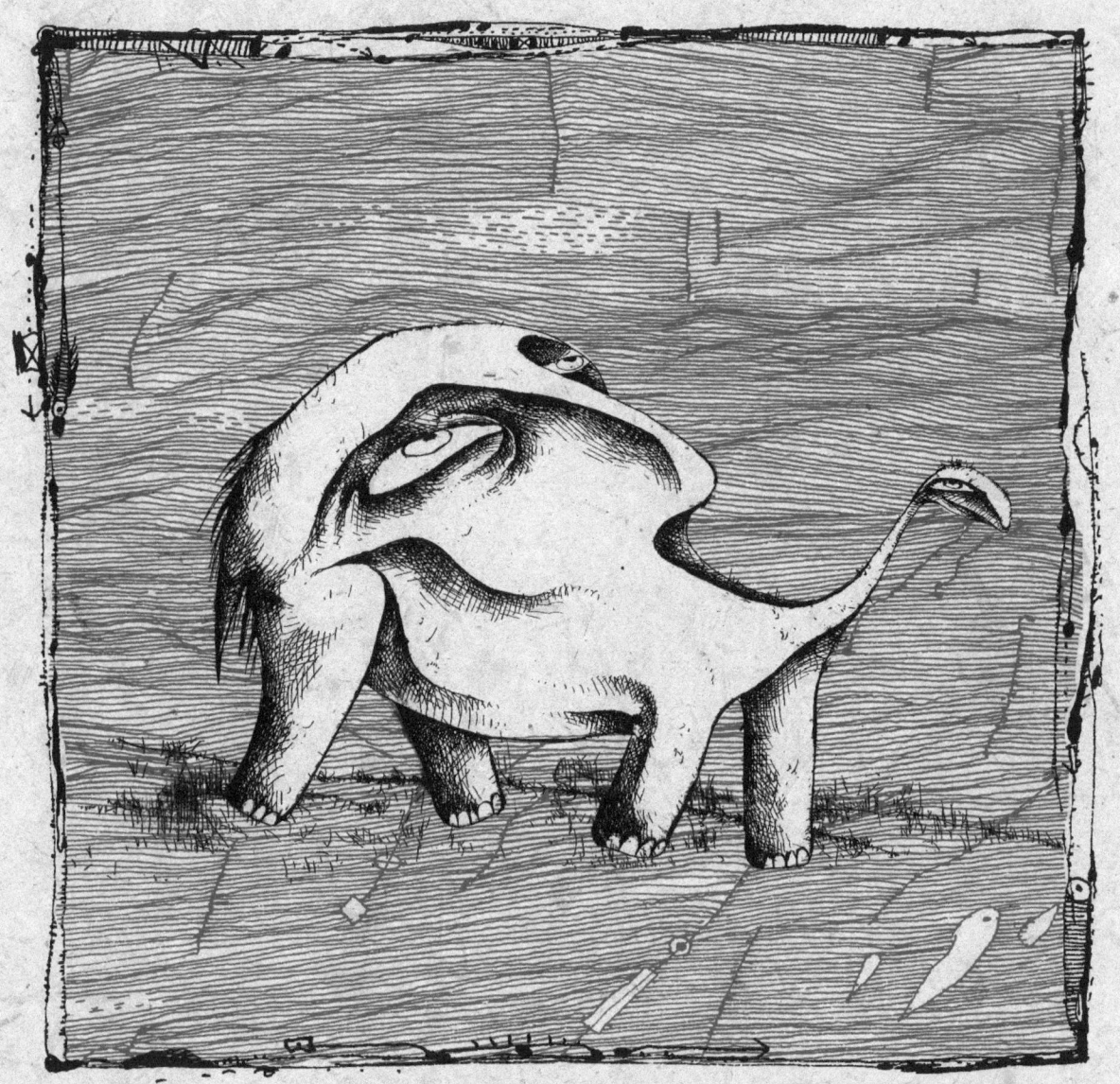

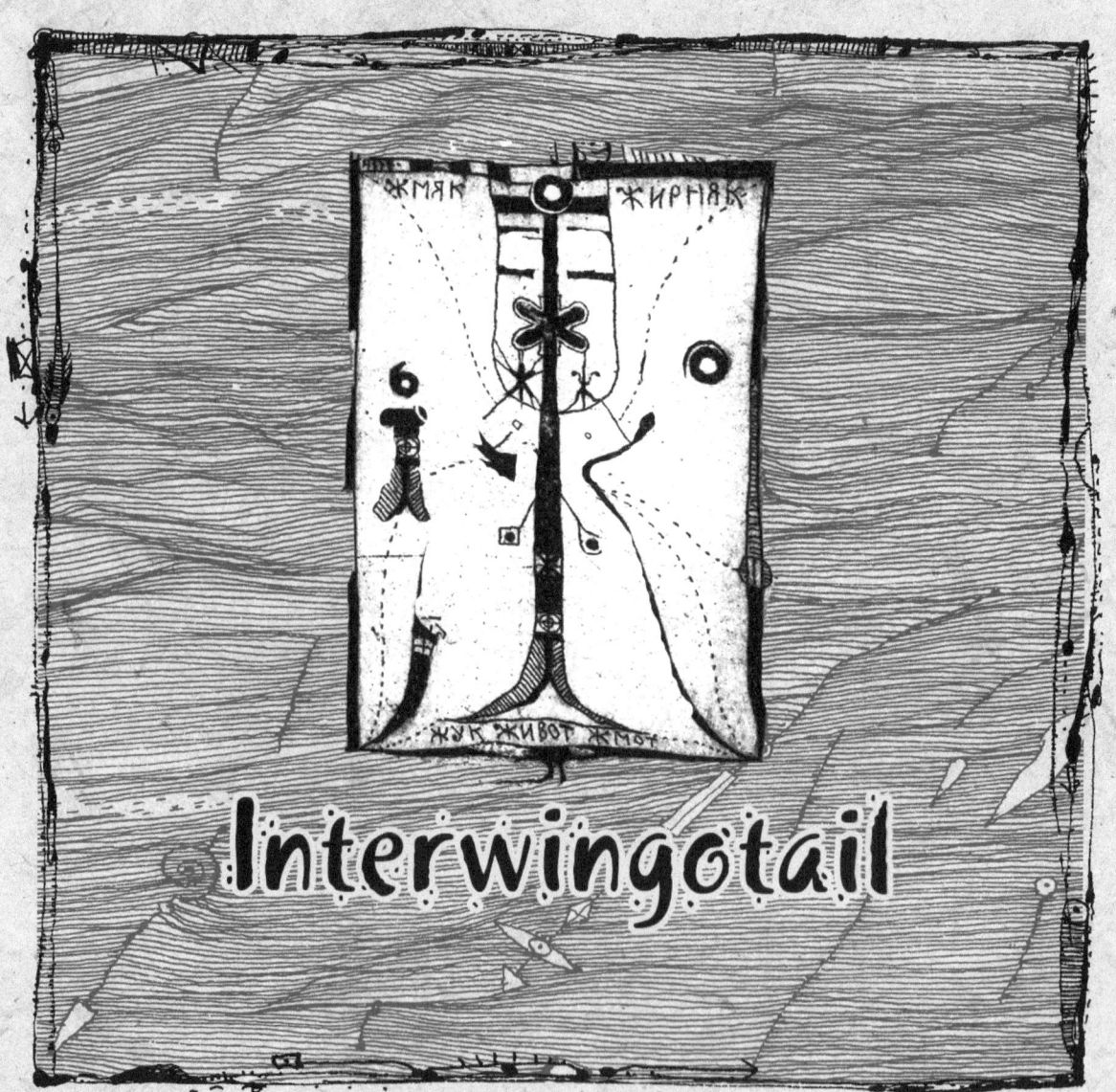

Interwingotail

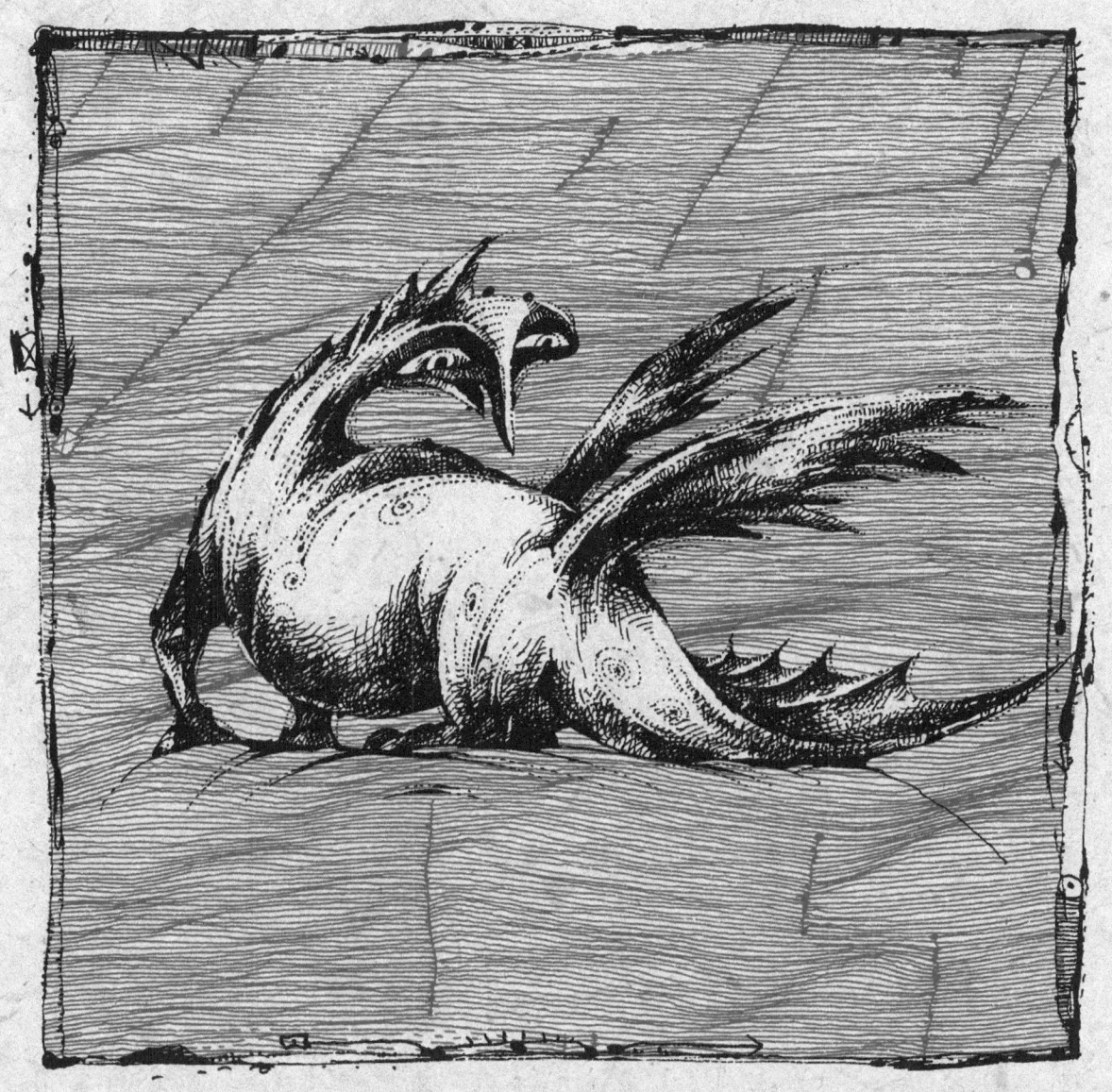

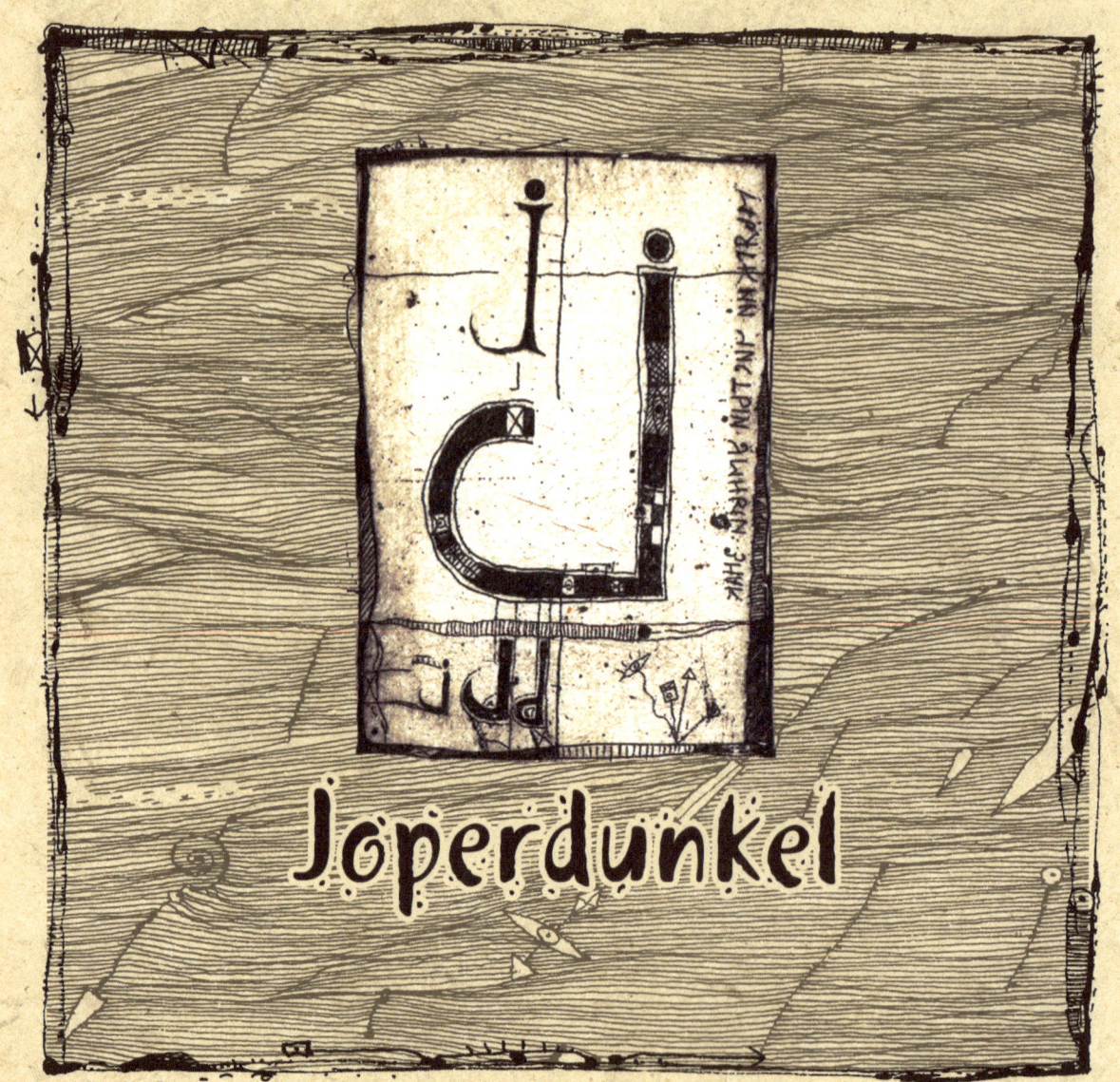

Joperdunkel

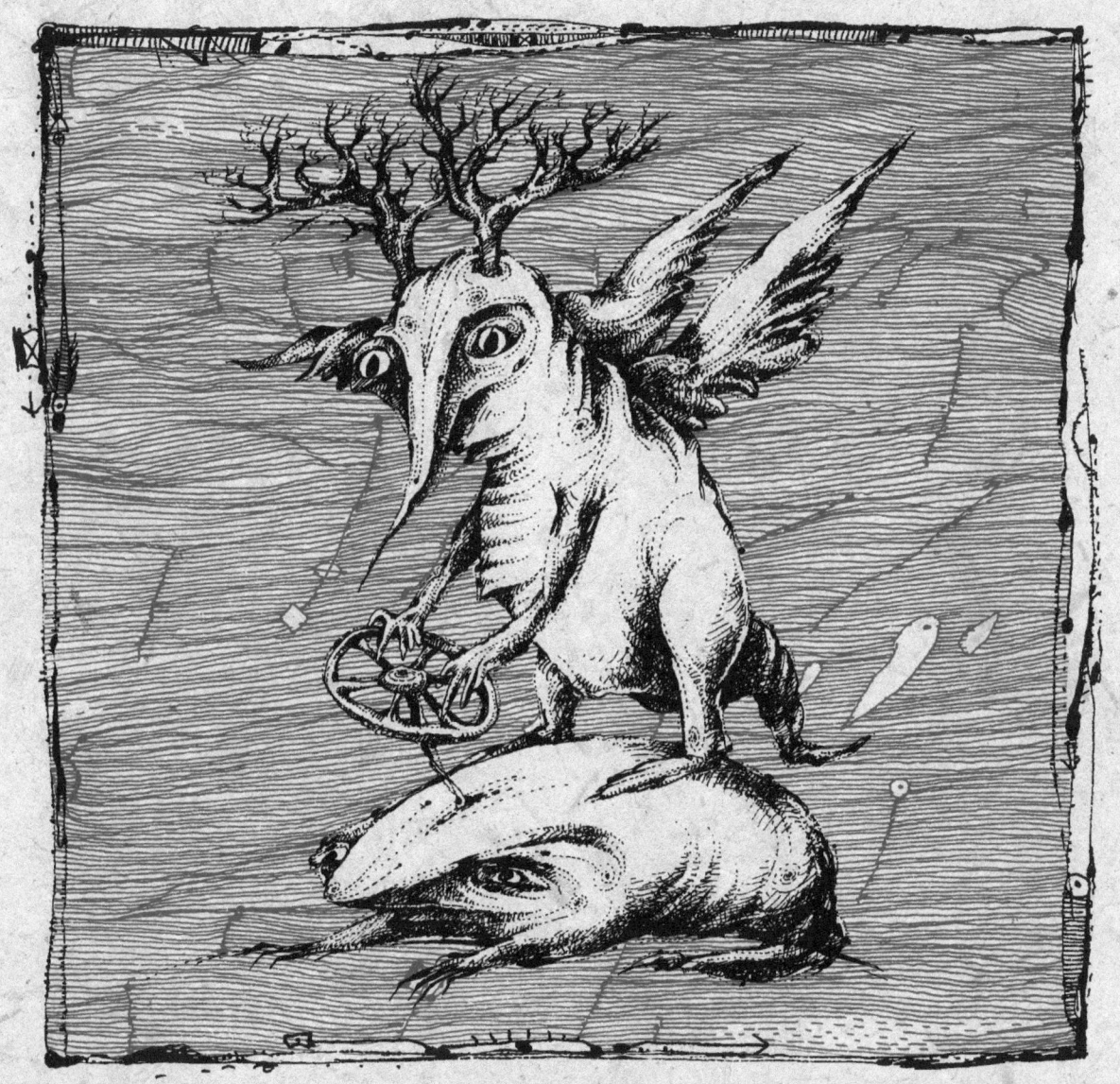

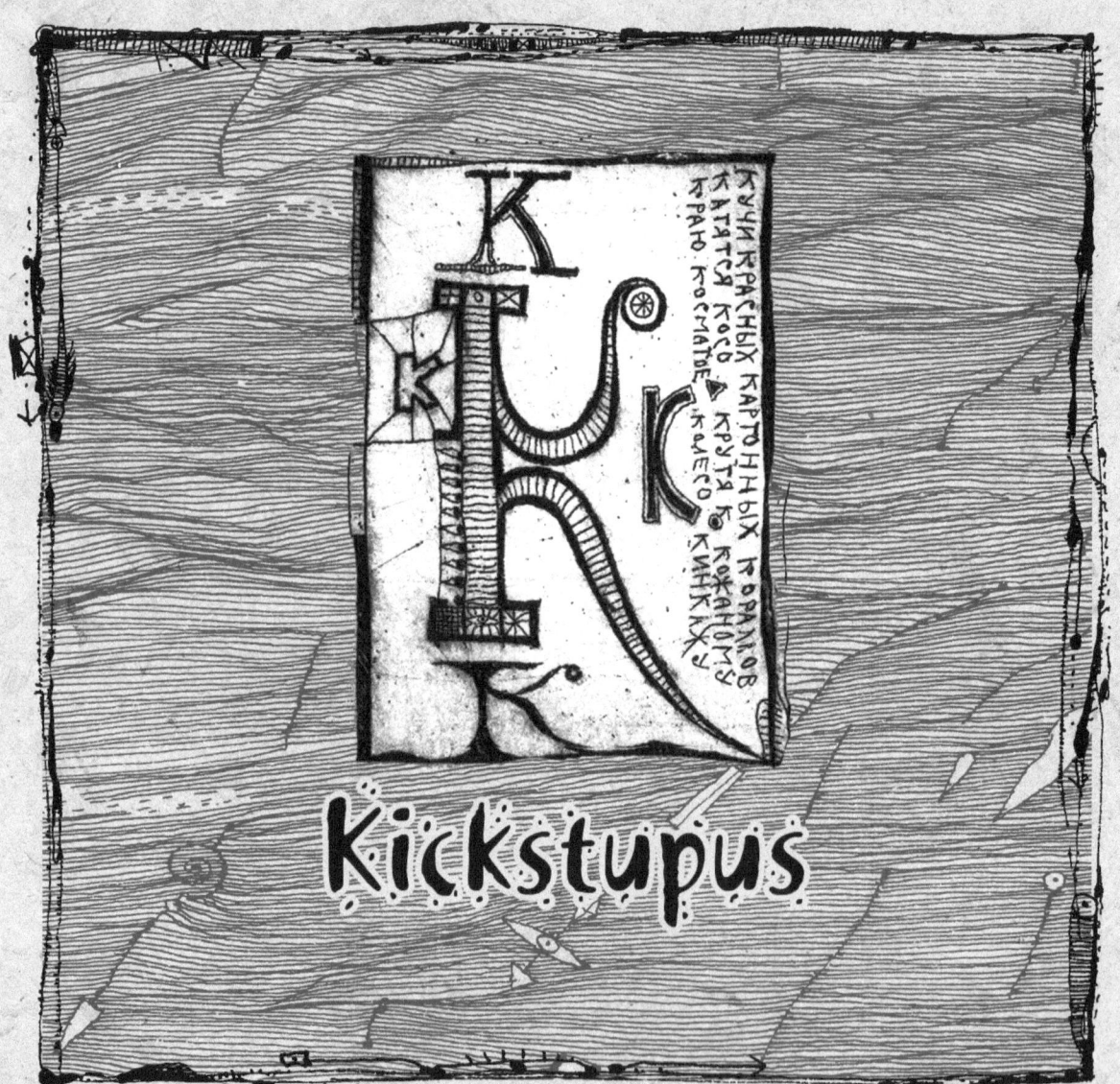

Kickstupus

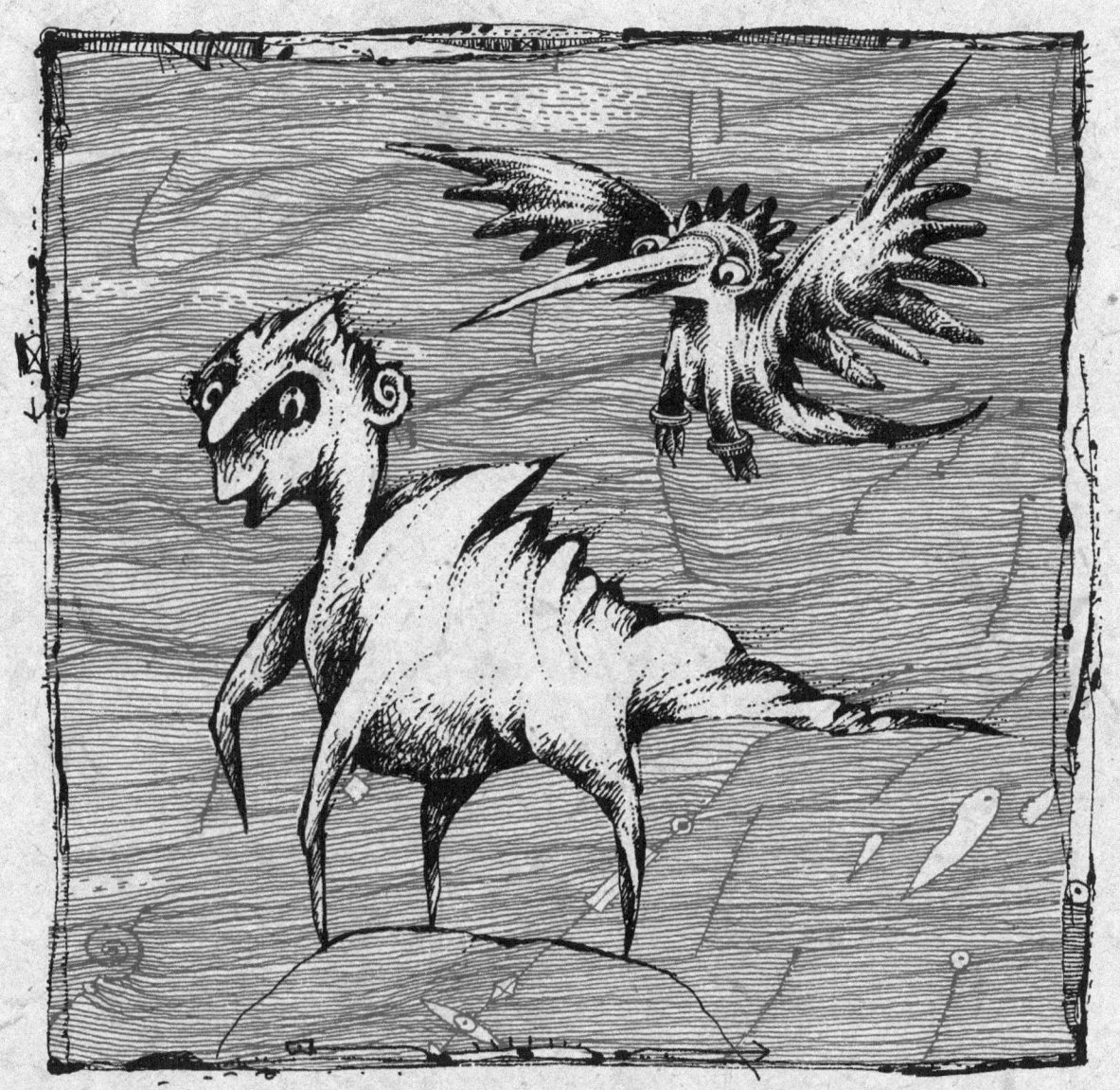

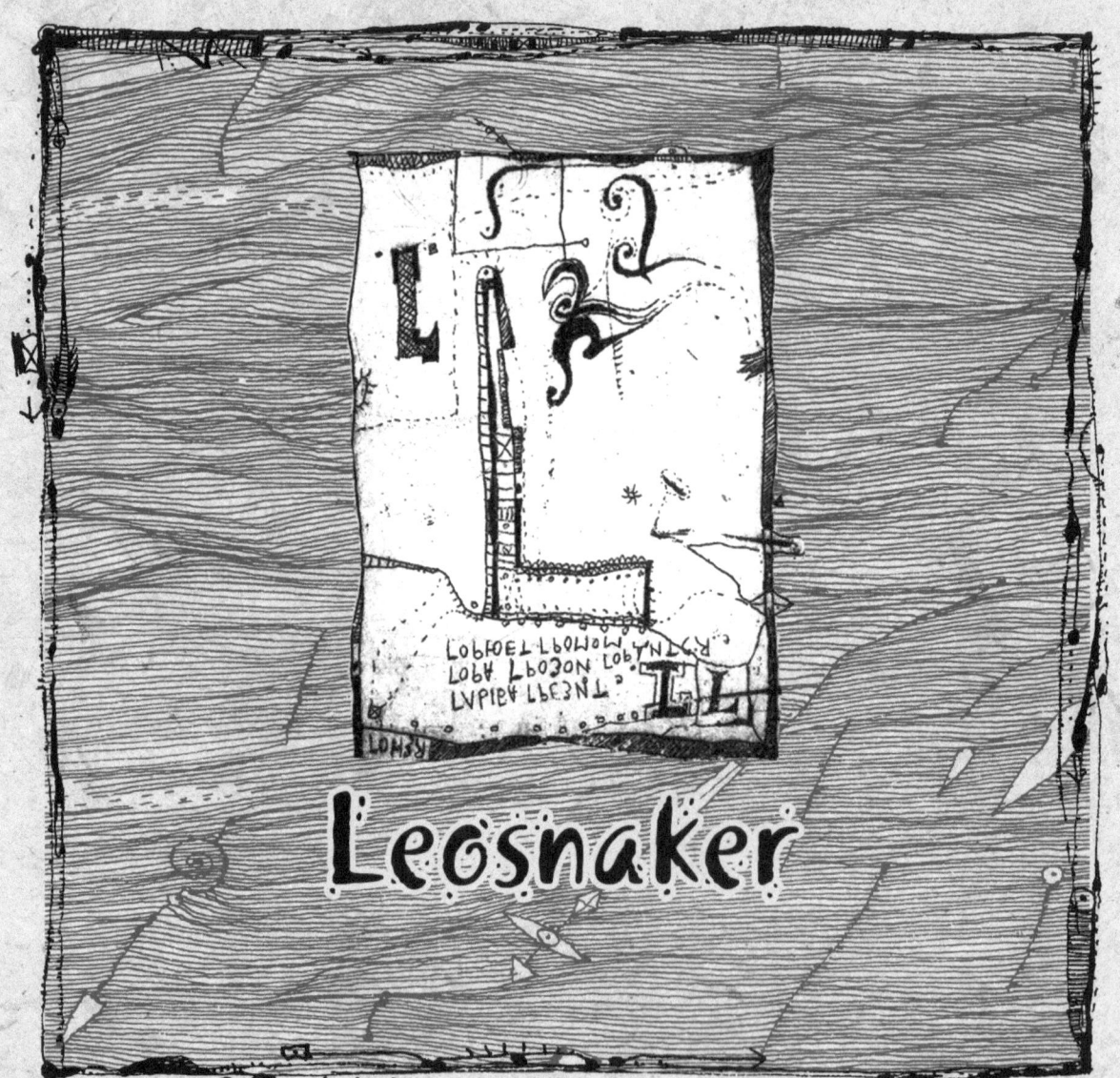

Leosnaker

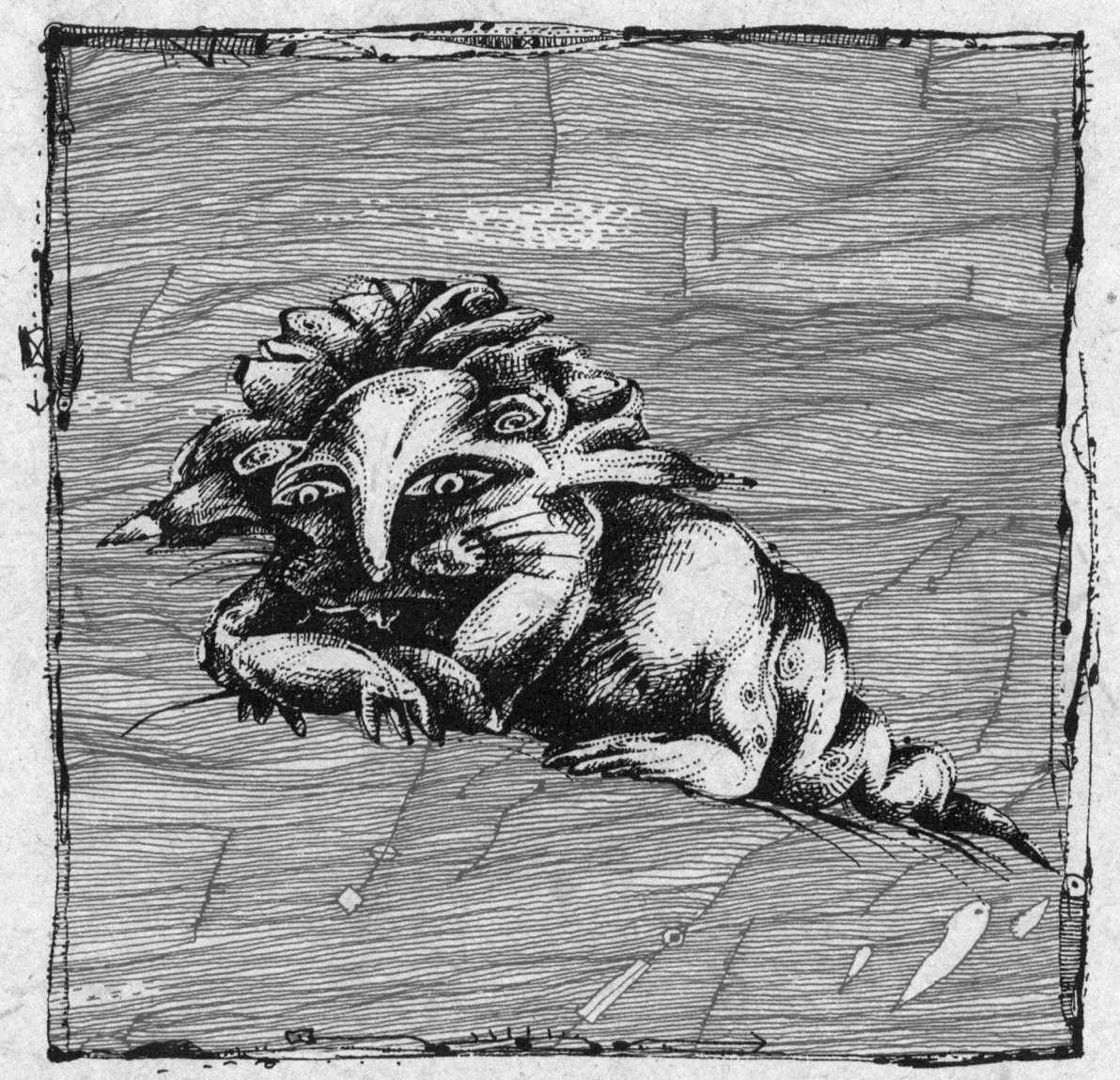

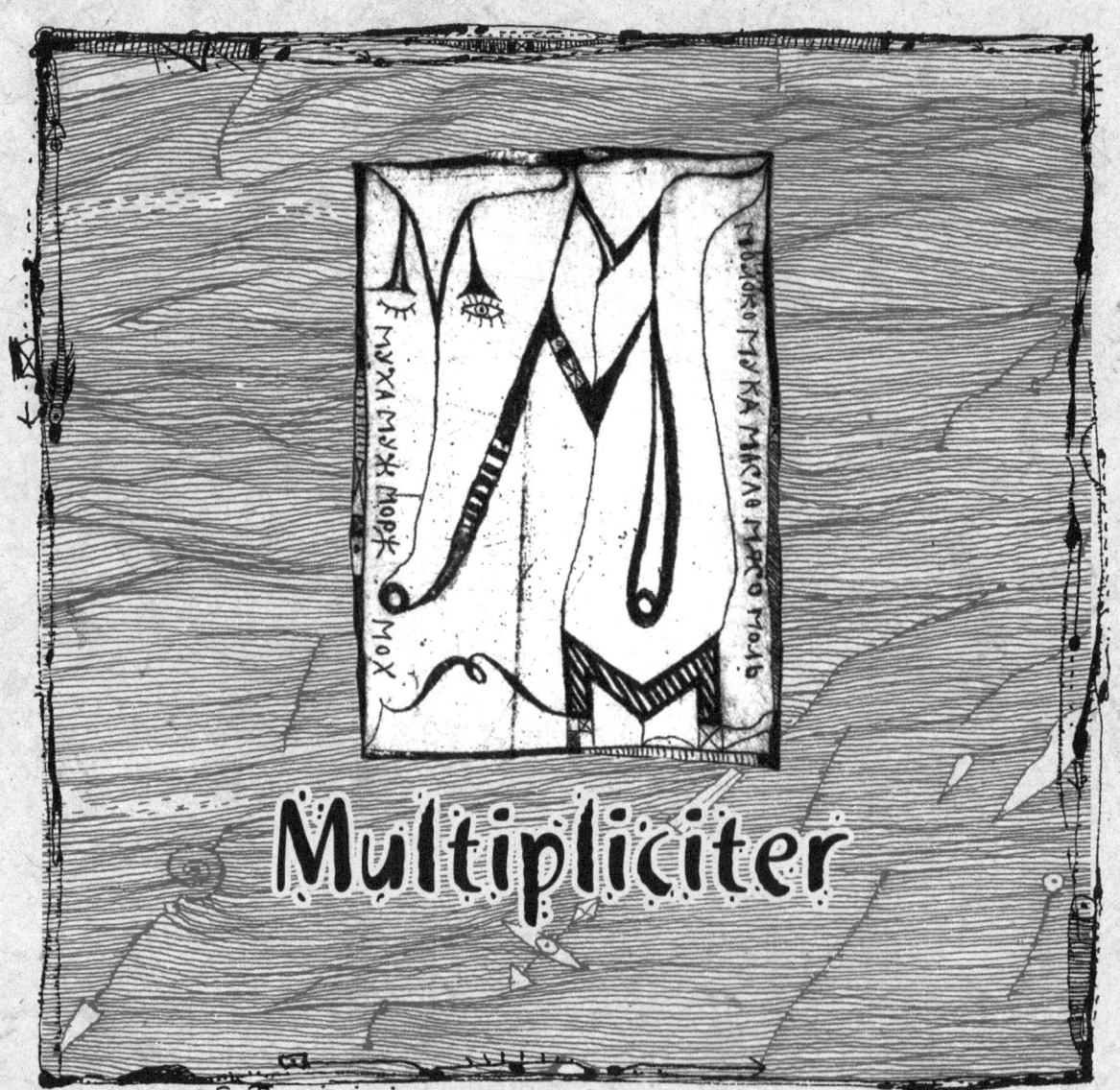

Multipliciter

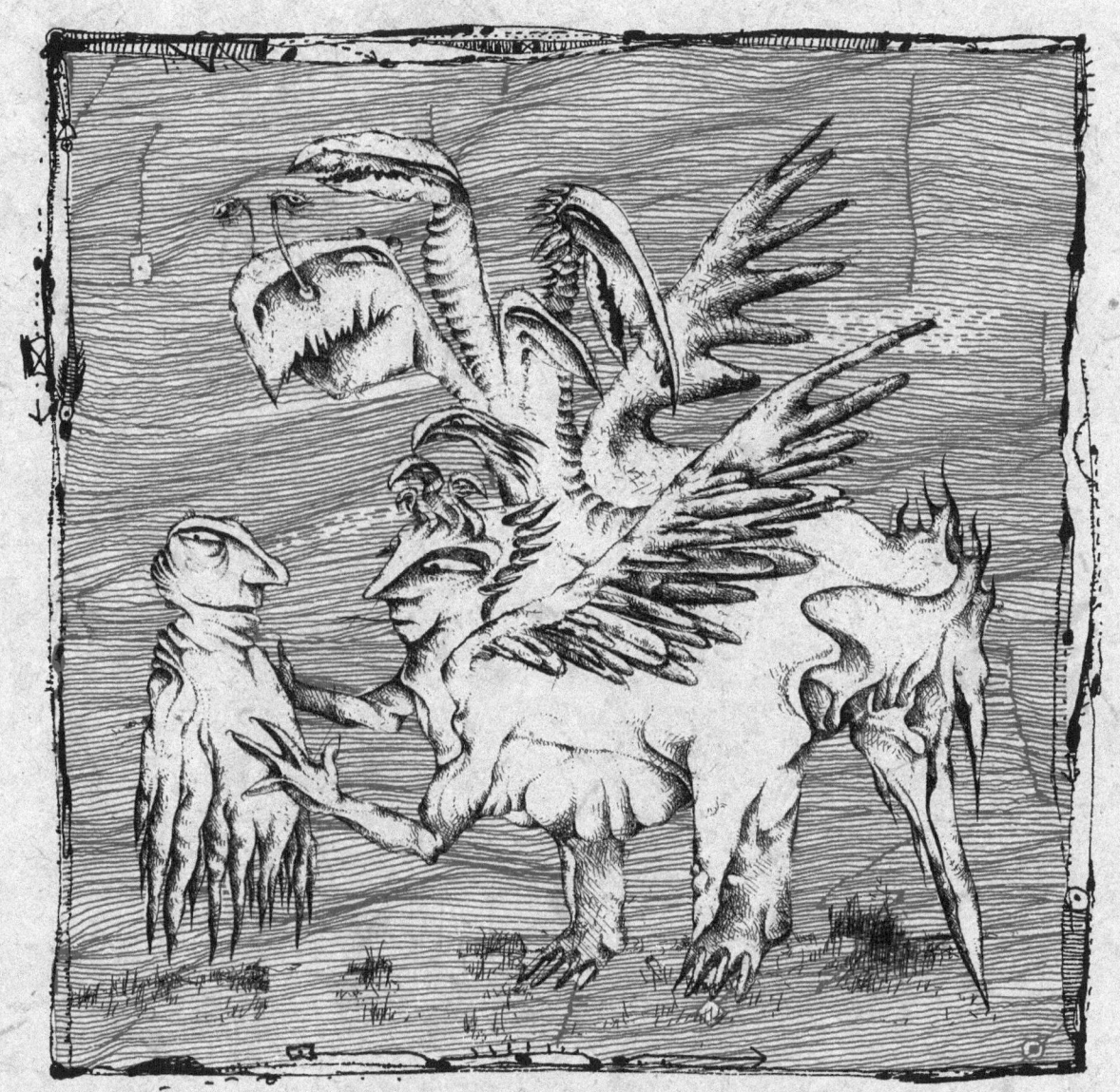

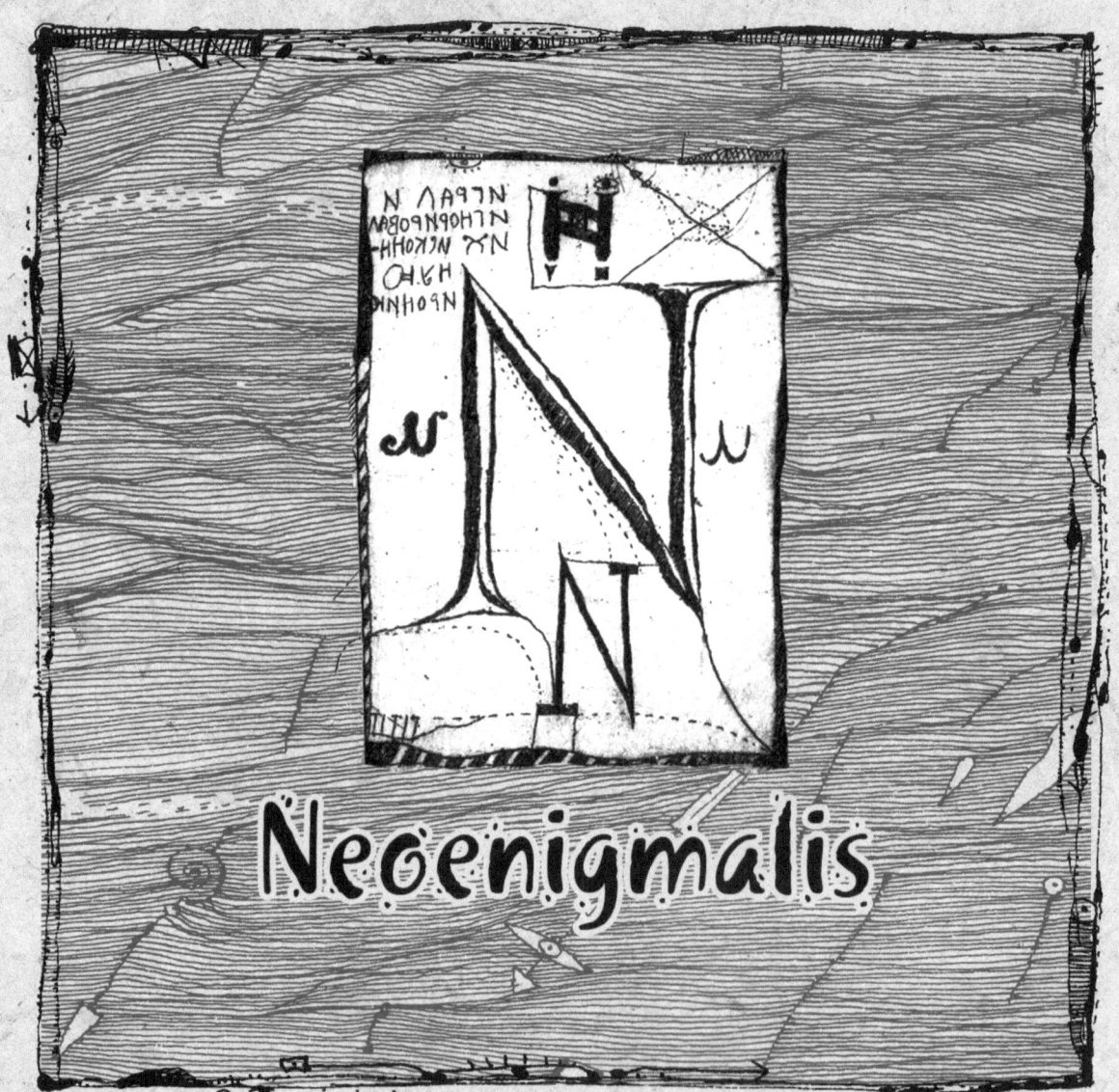

Neoenigmalis

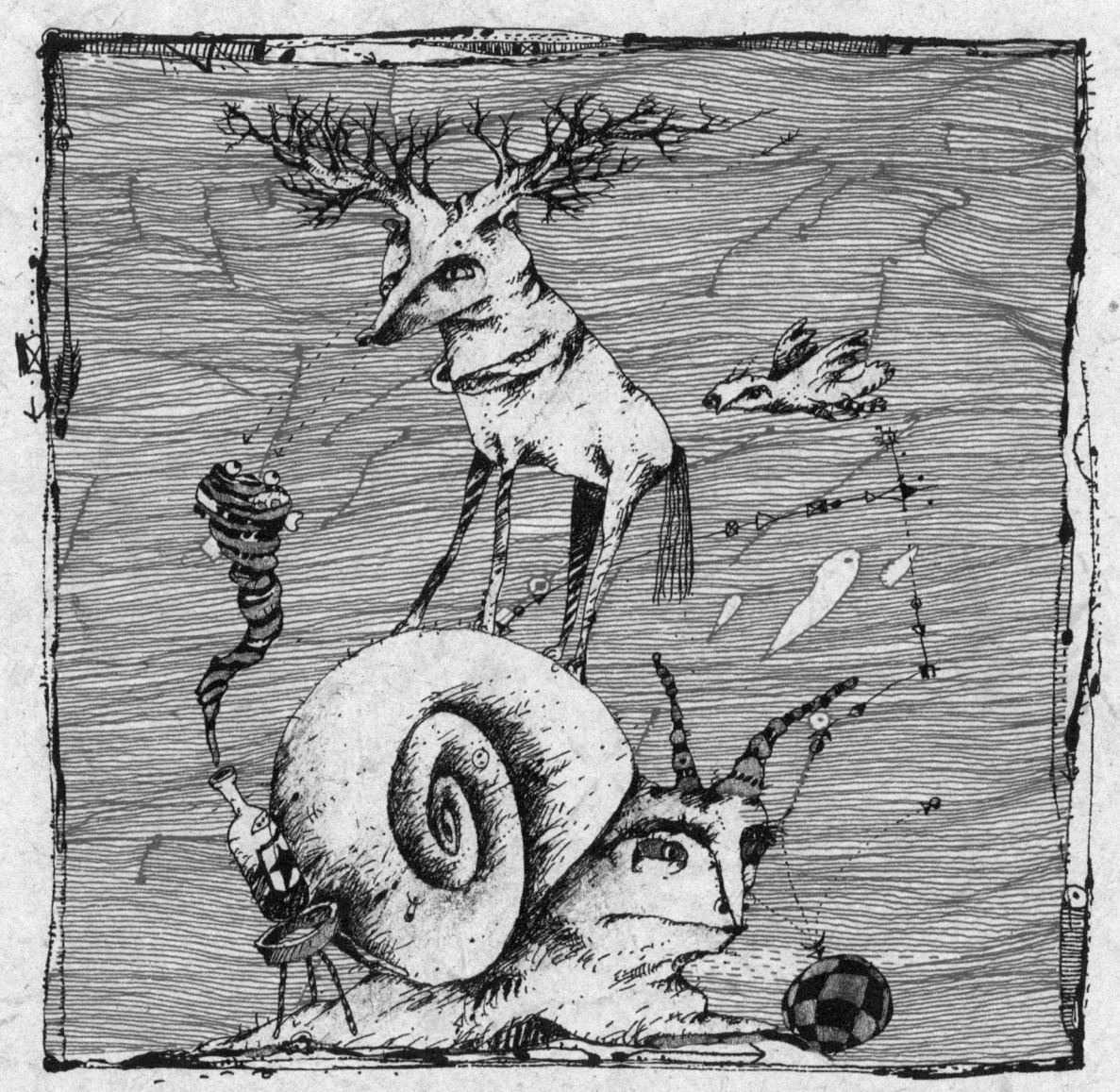

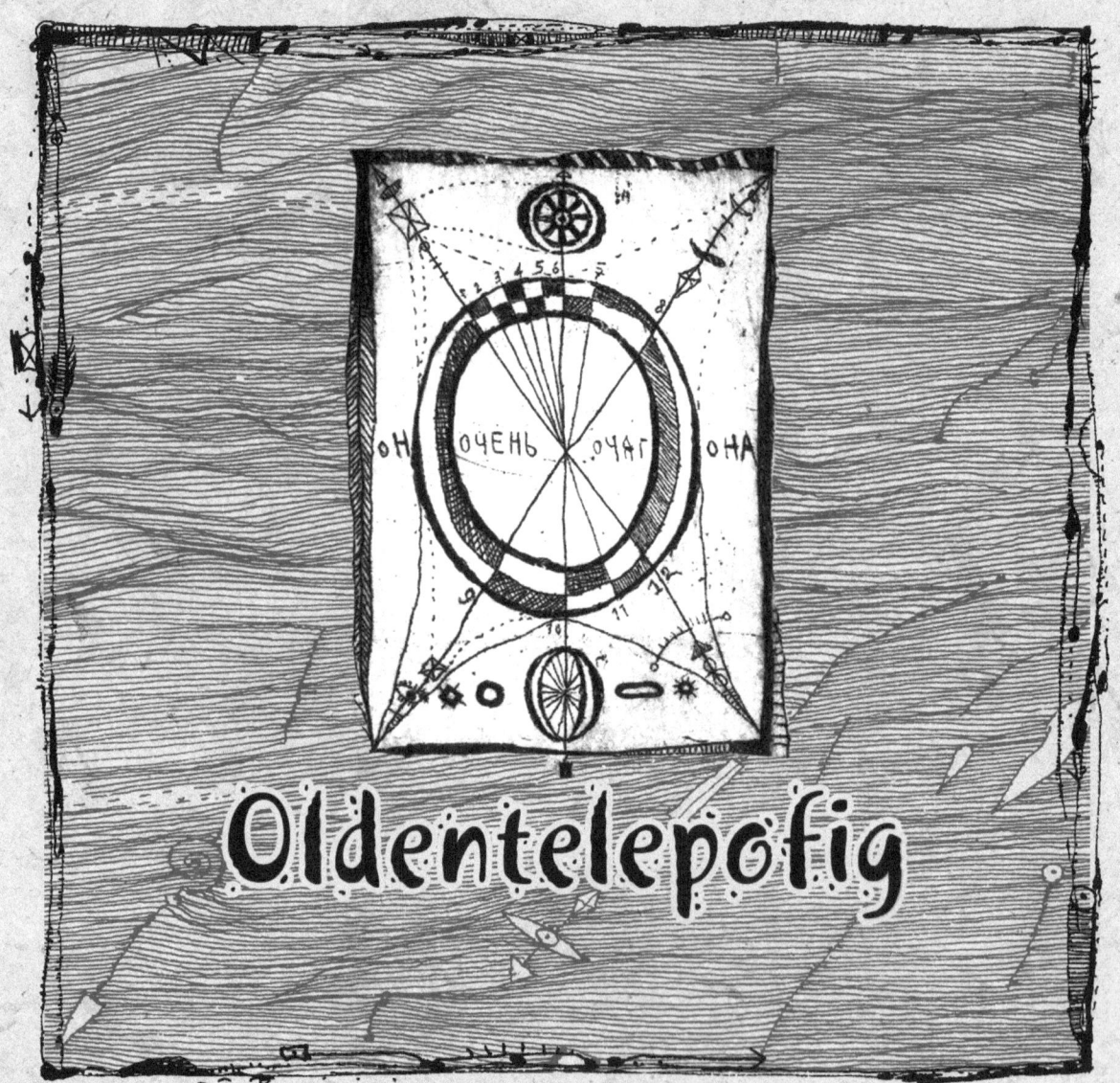

Oldentelepofig

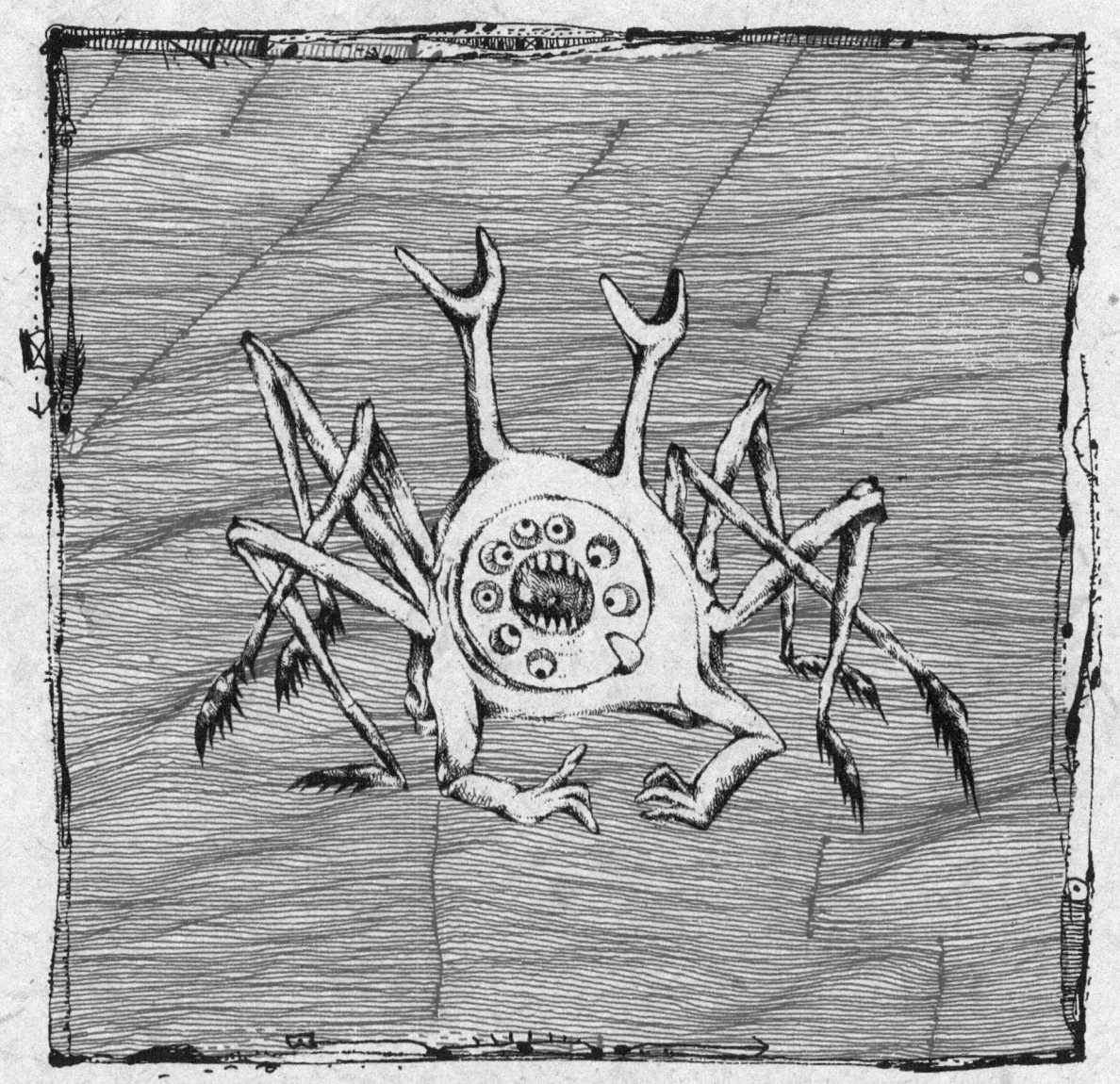

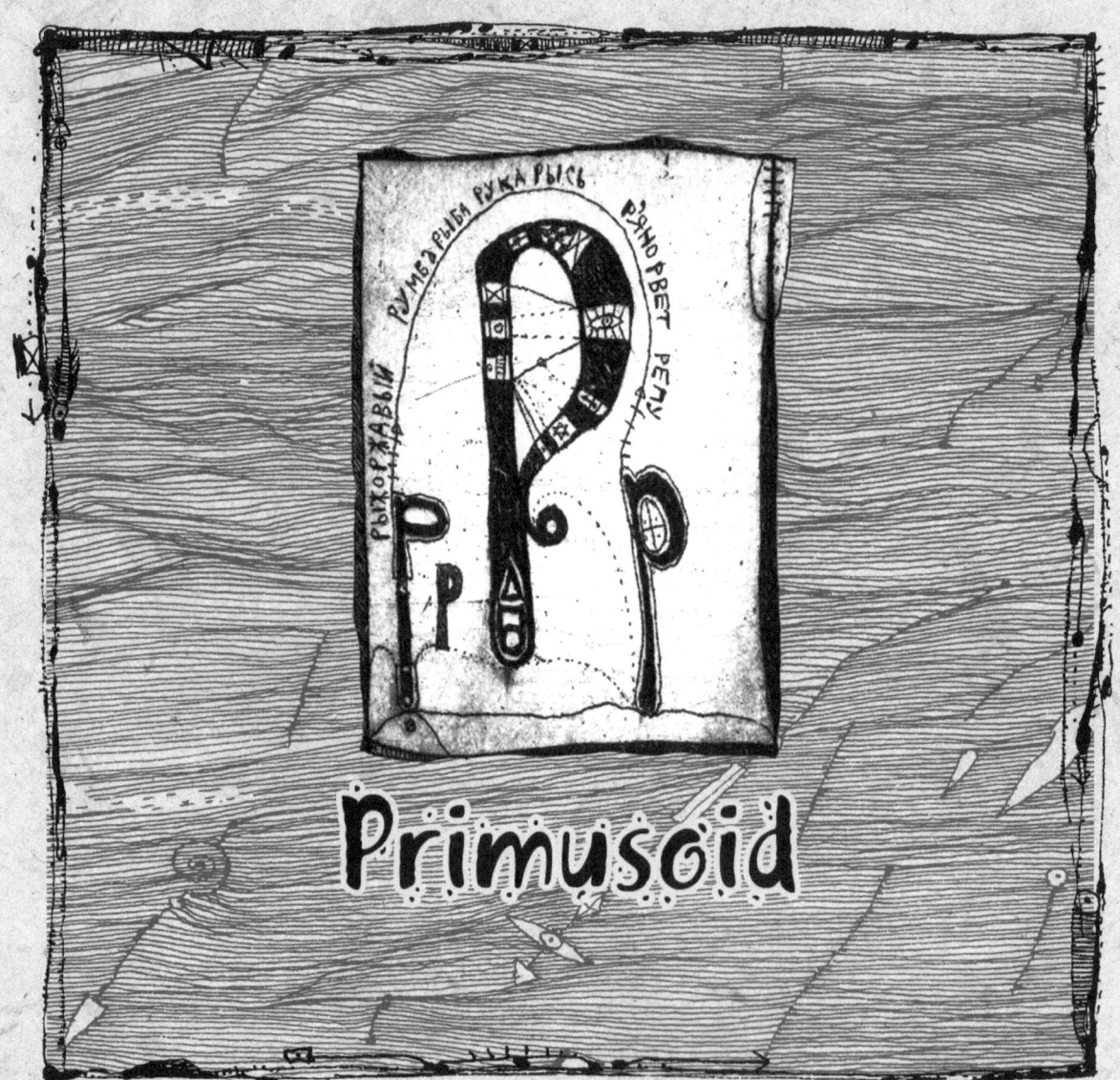

Primusoid

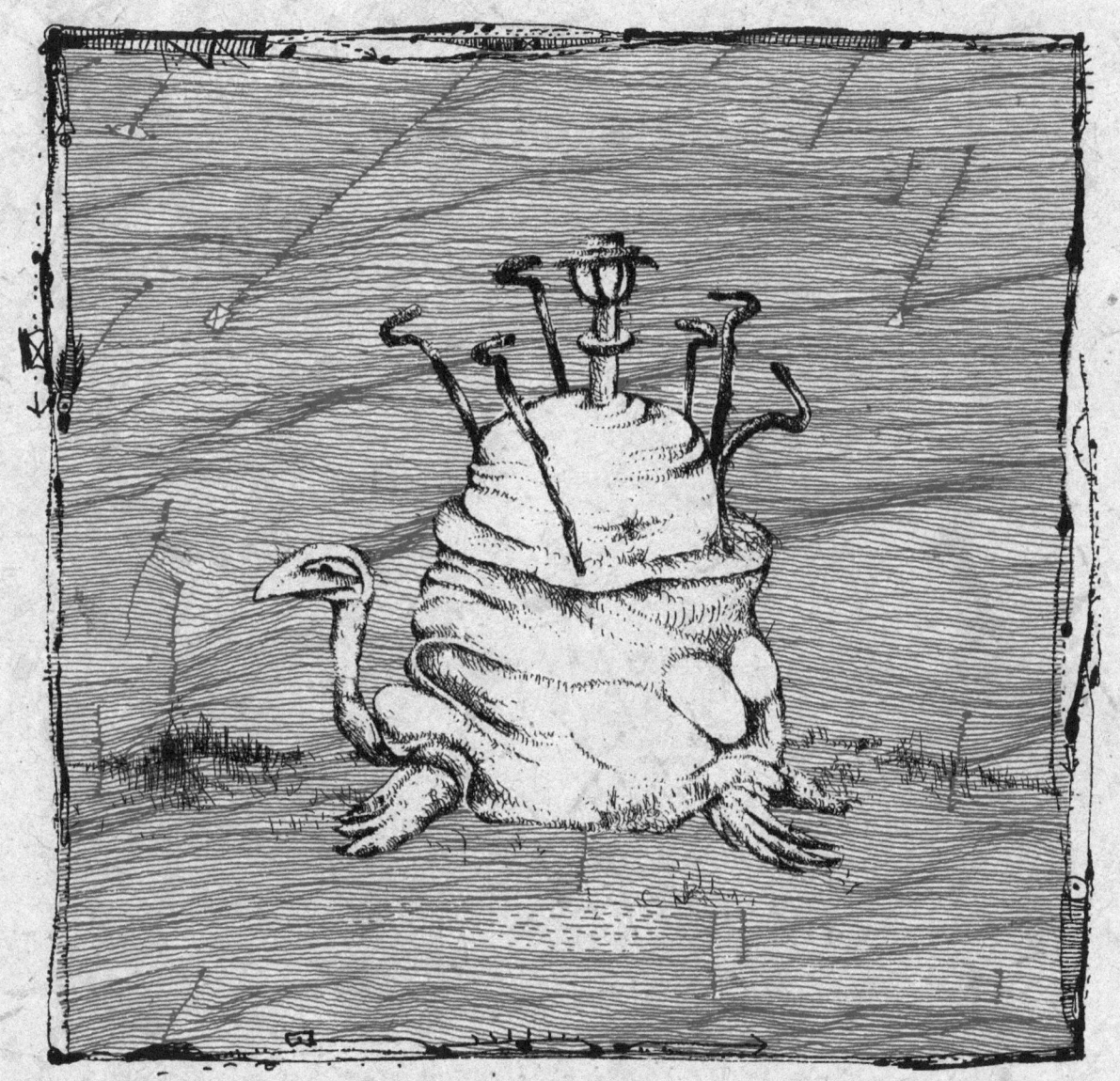

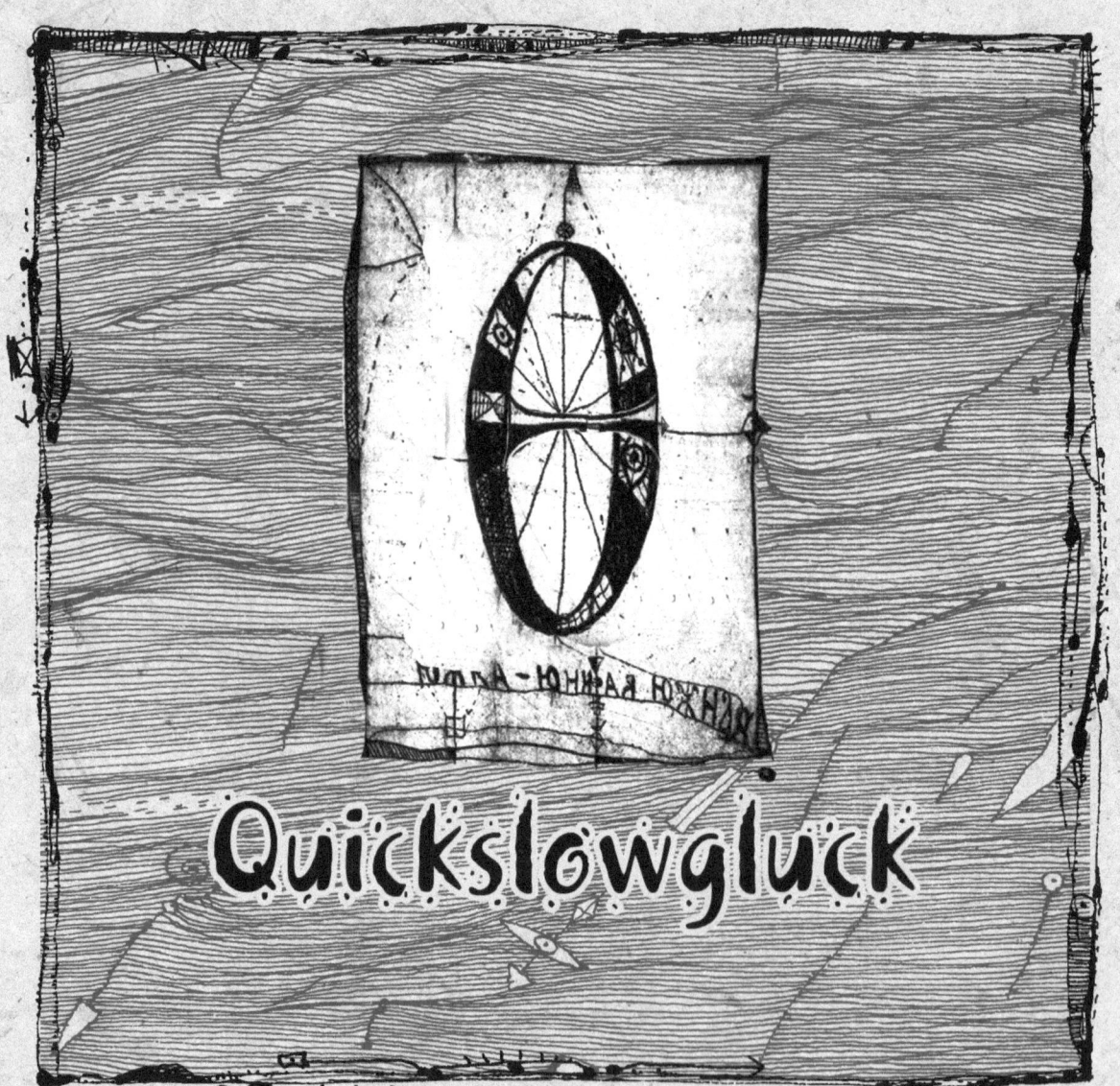

Quickslowgluck

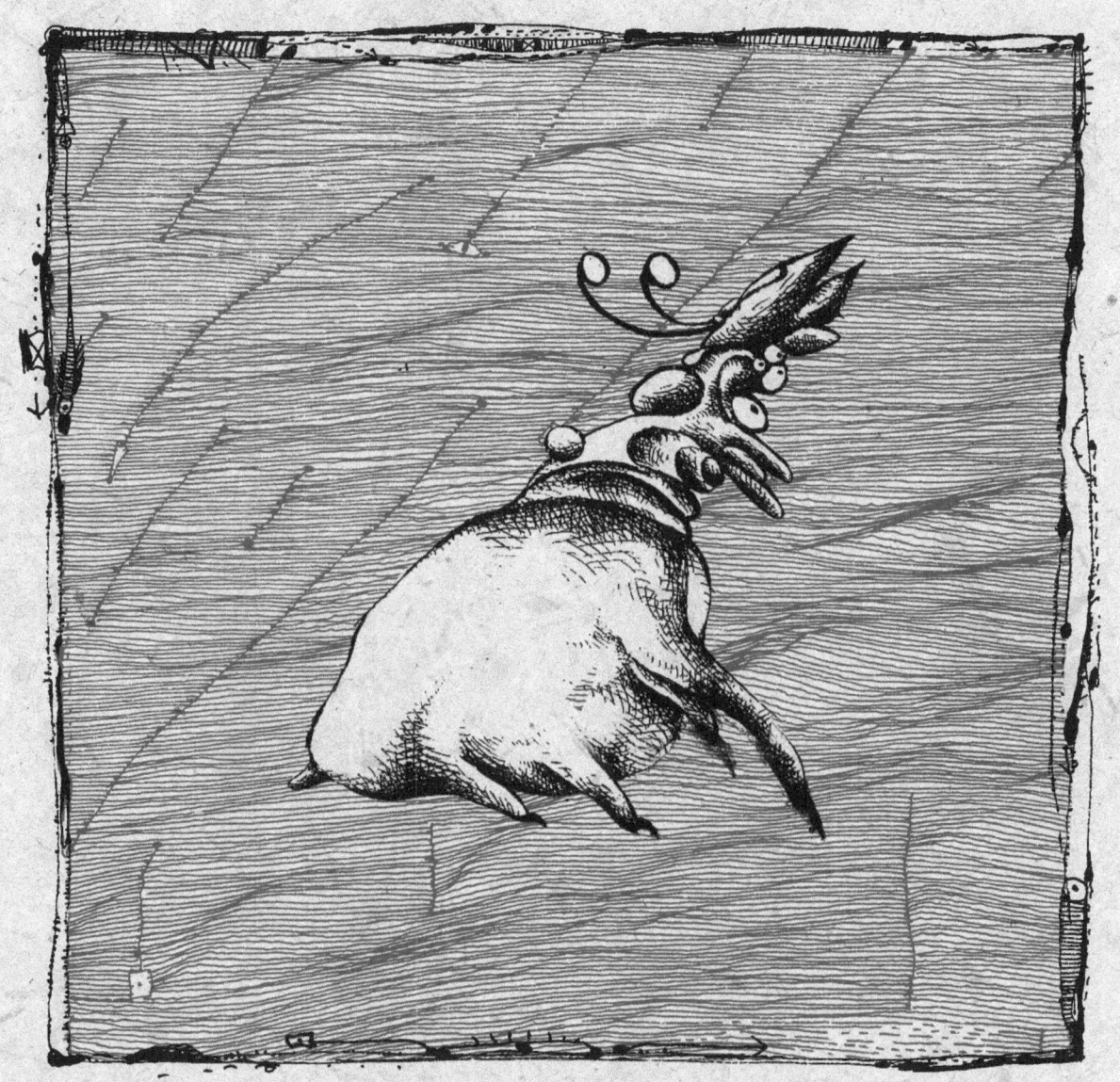

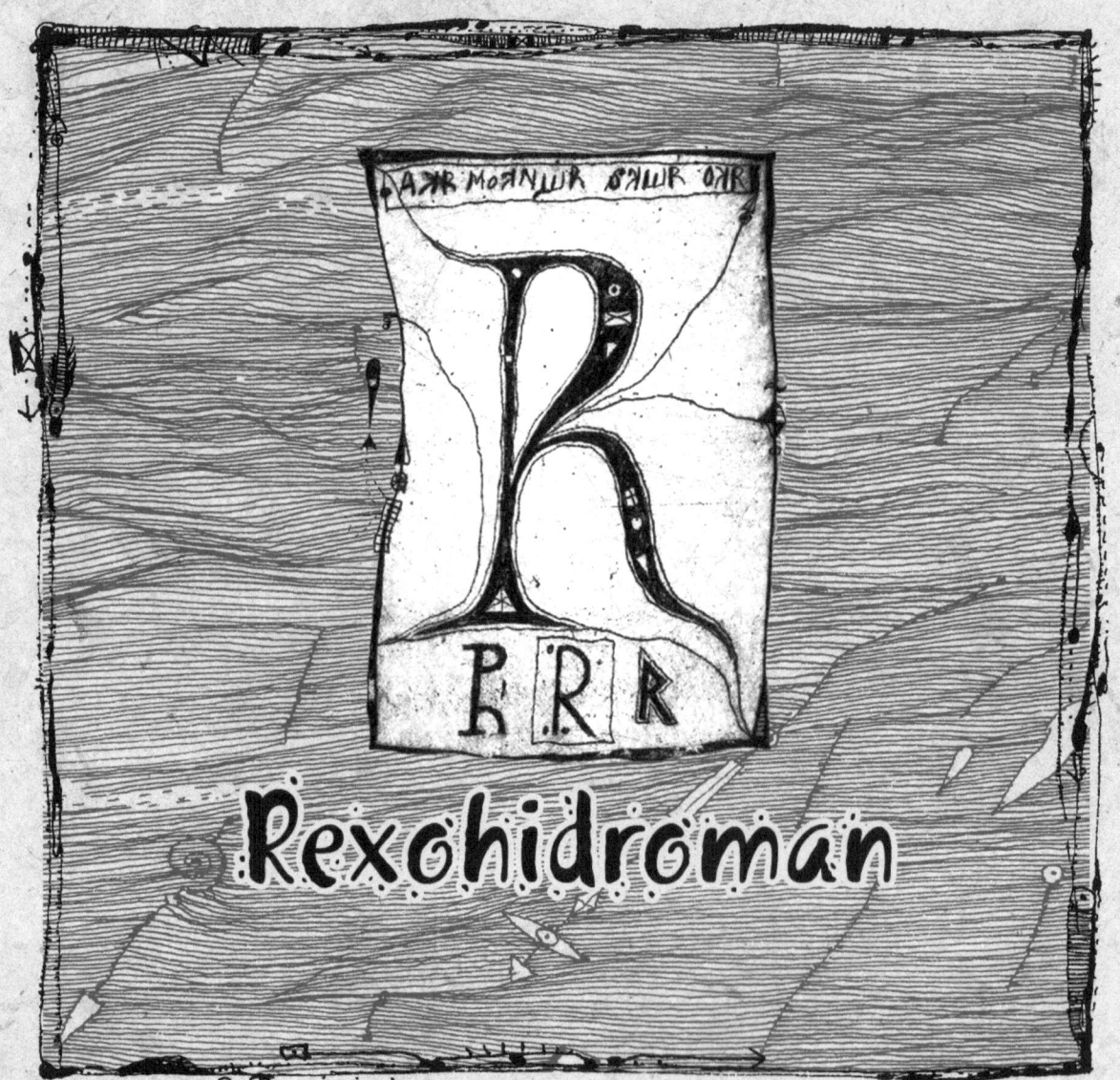

Rexohidroman

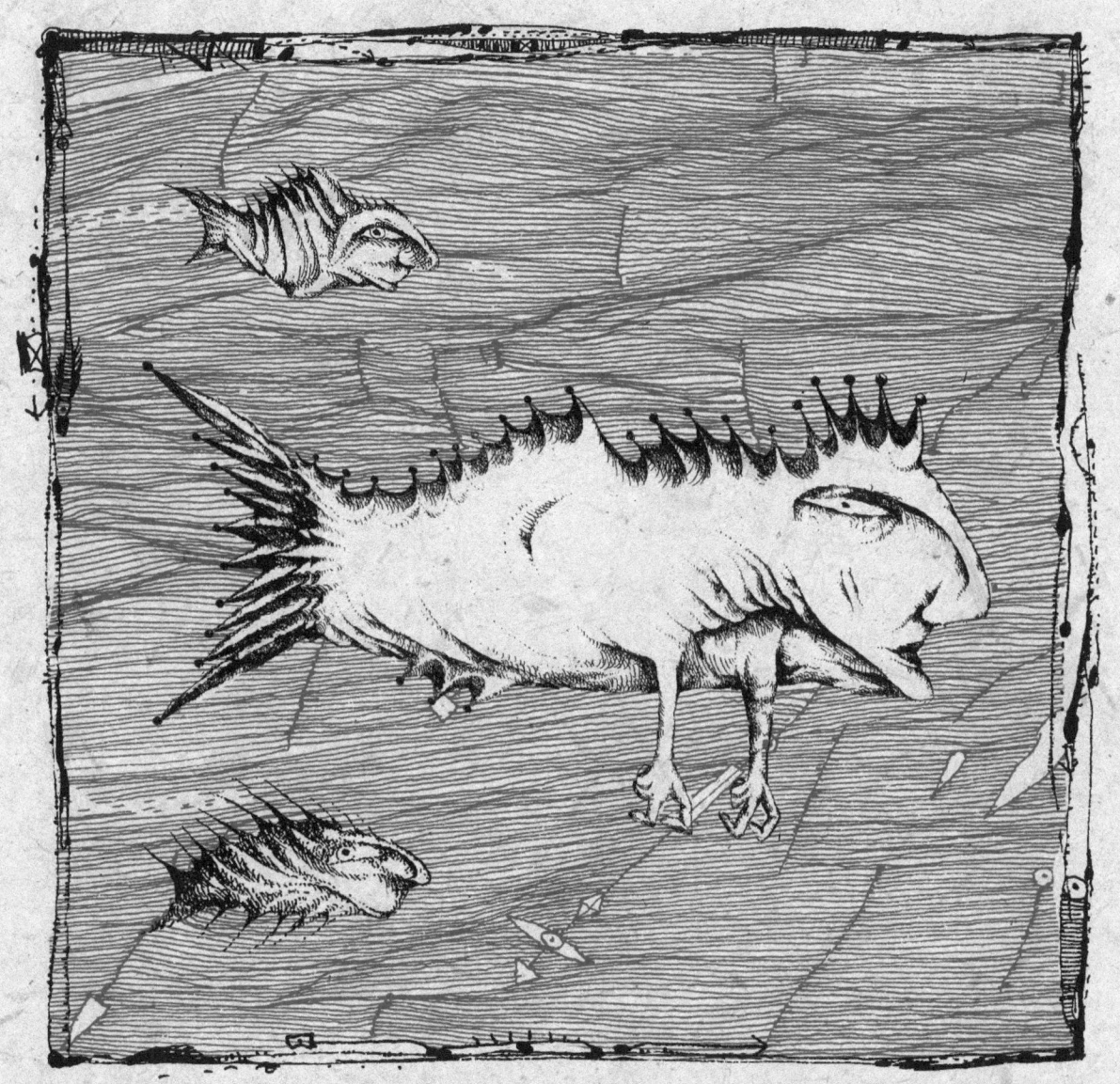

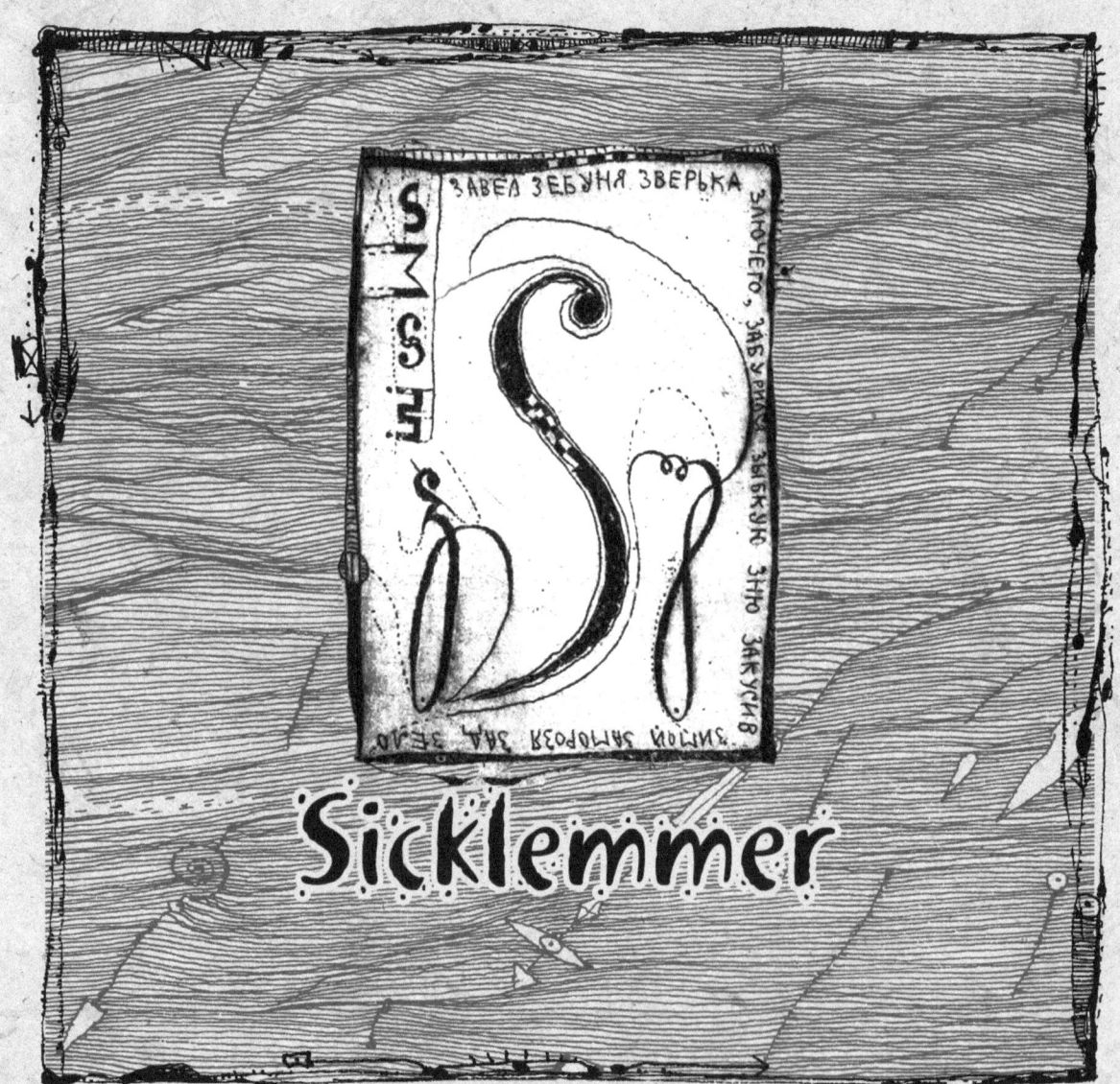

Sicklemmer

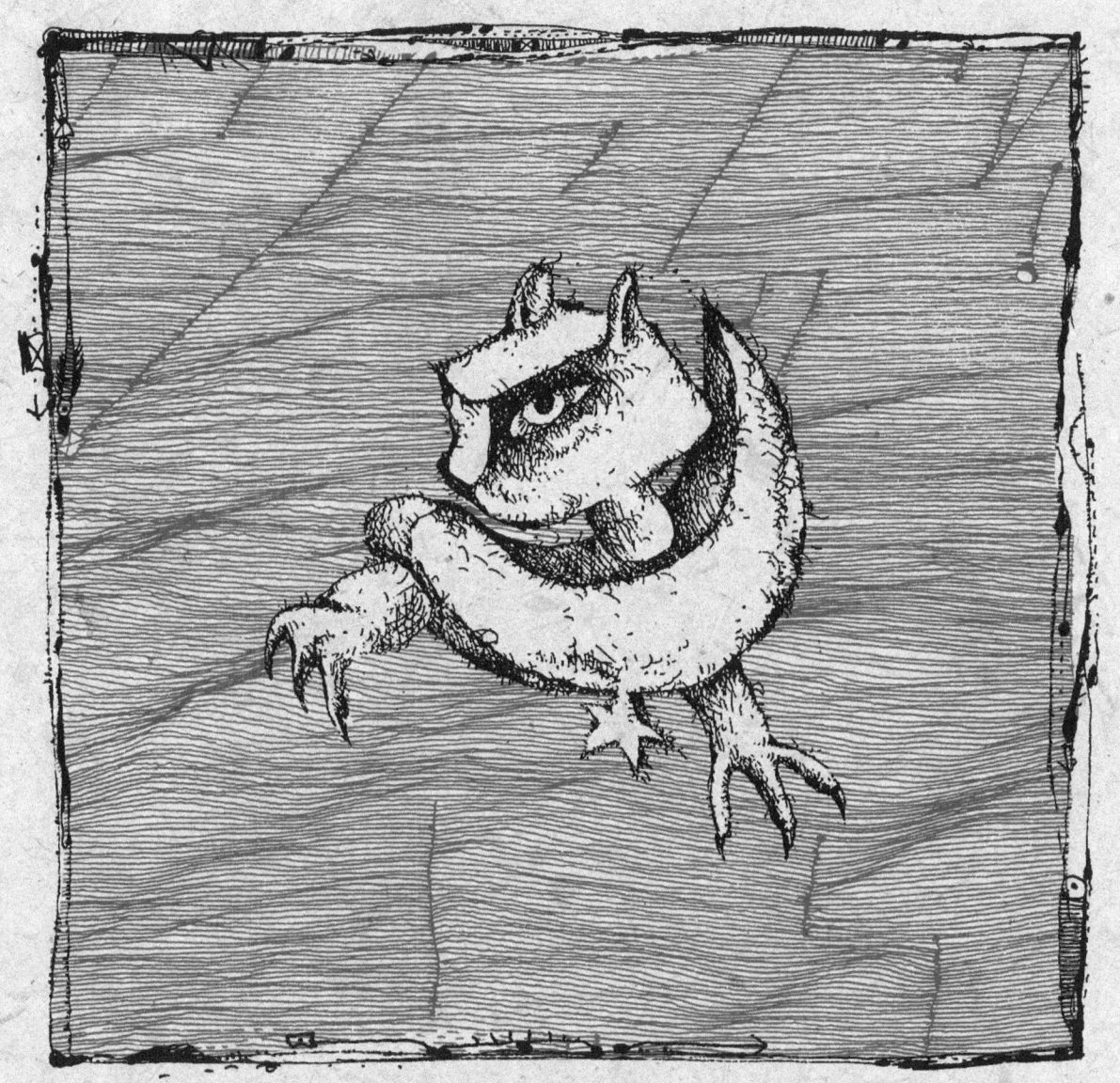

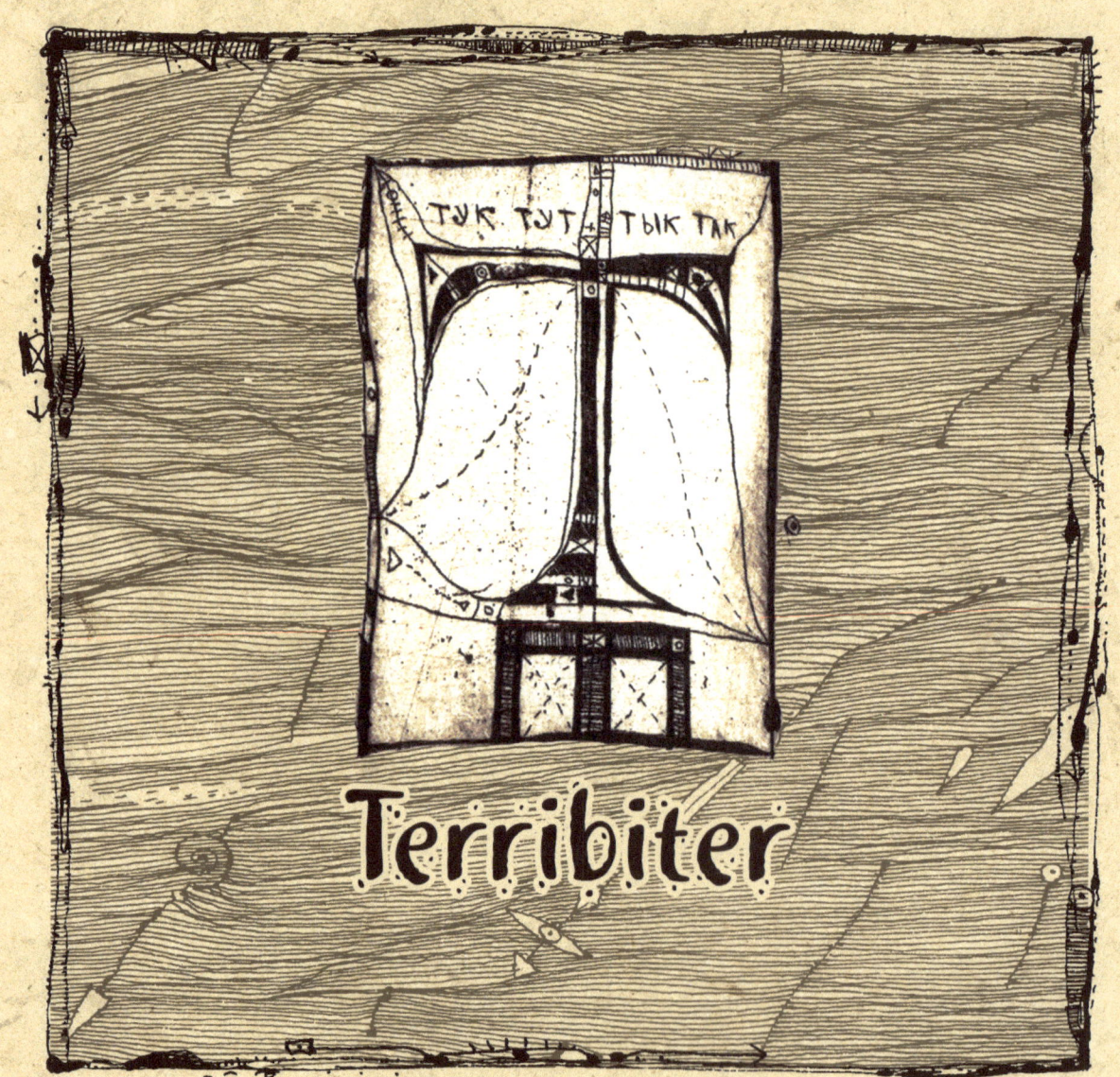

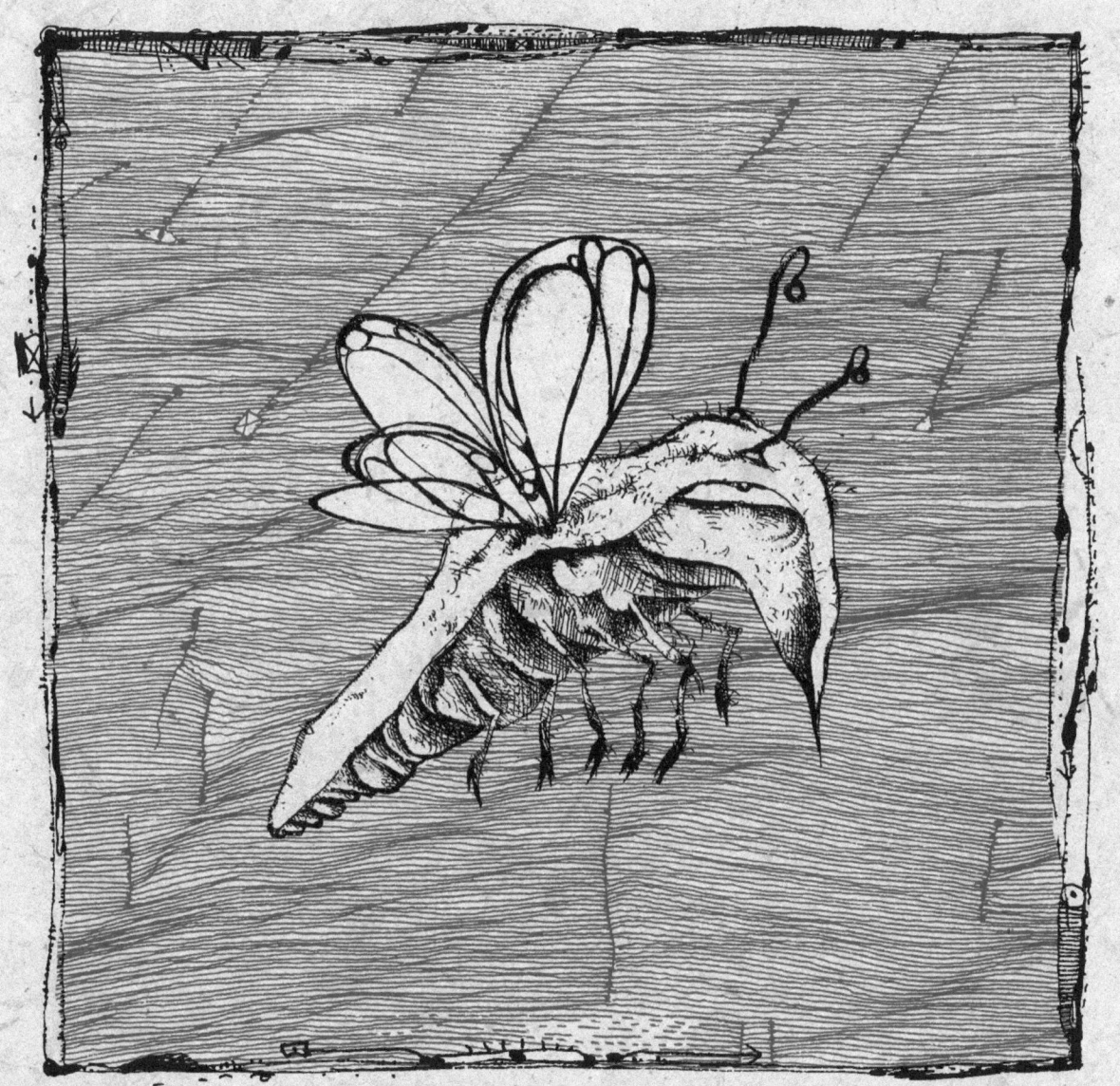

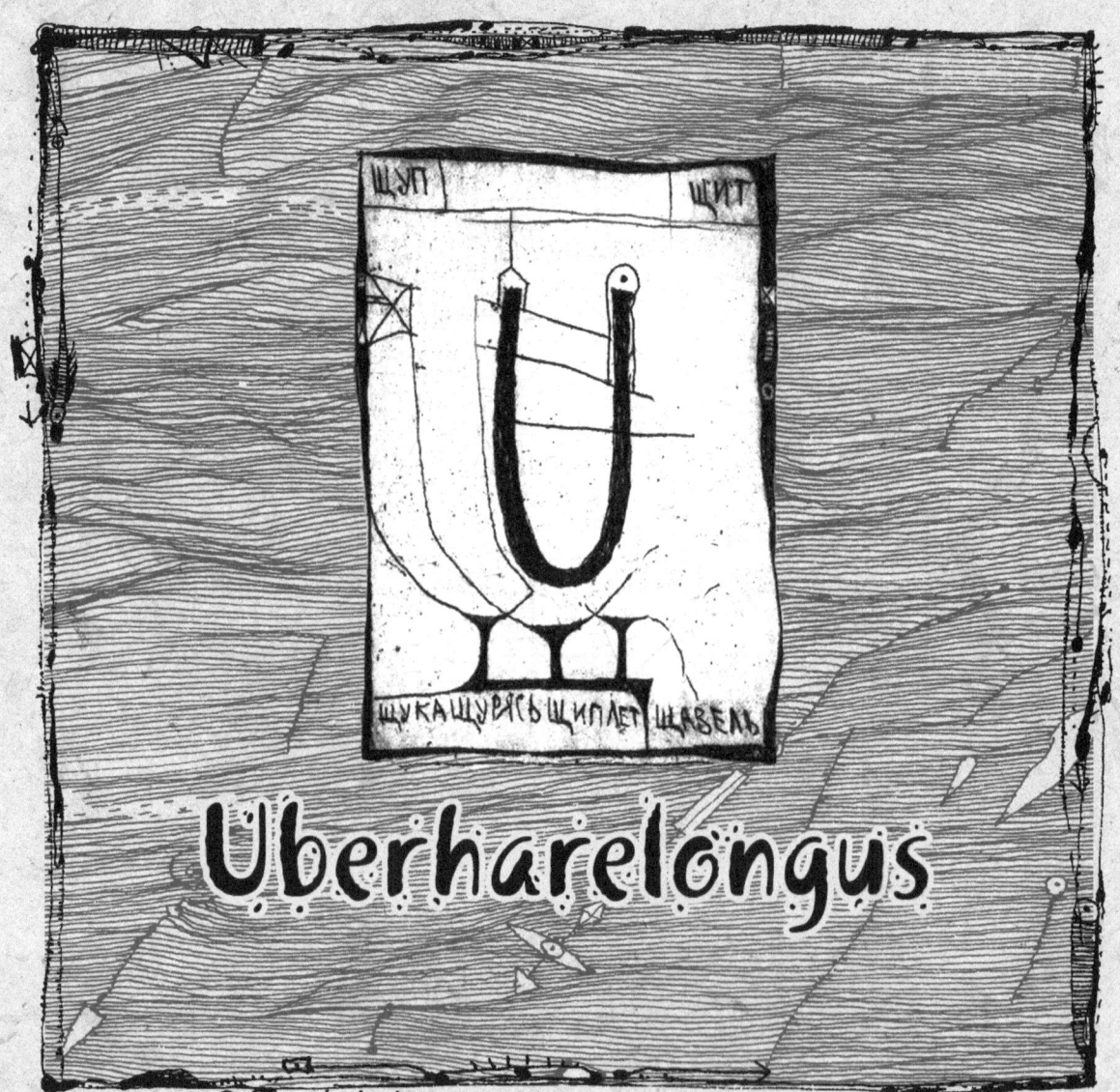

Uberharelongus

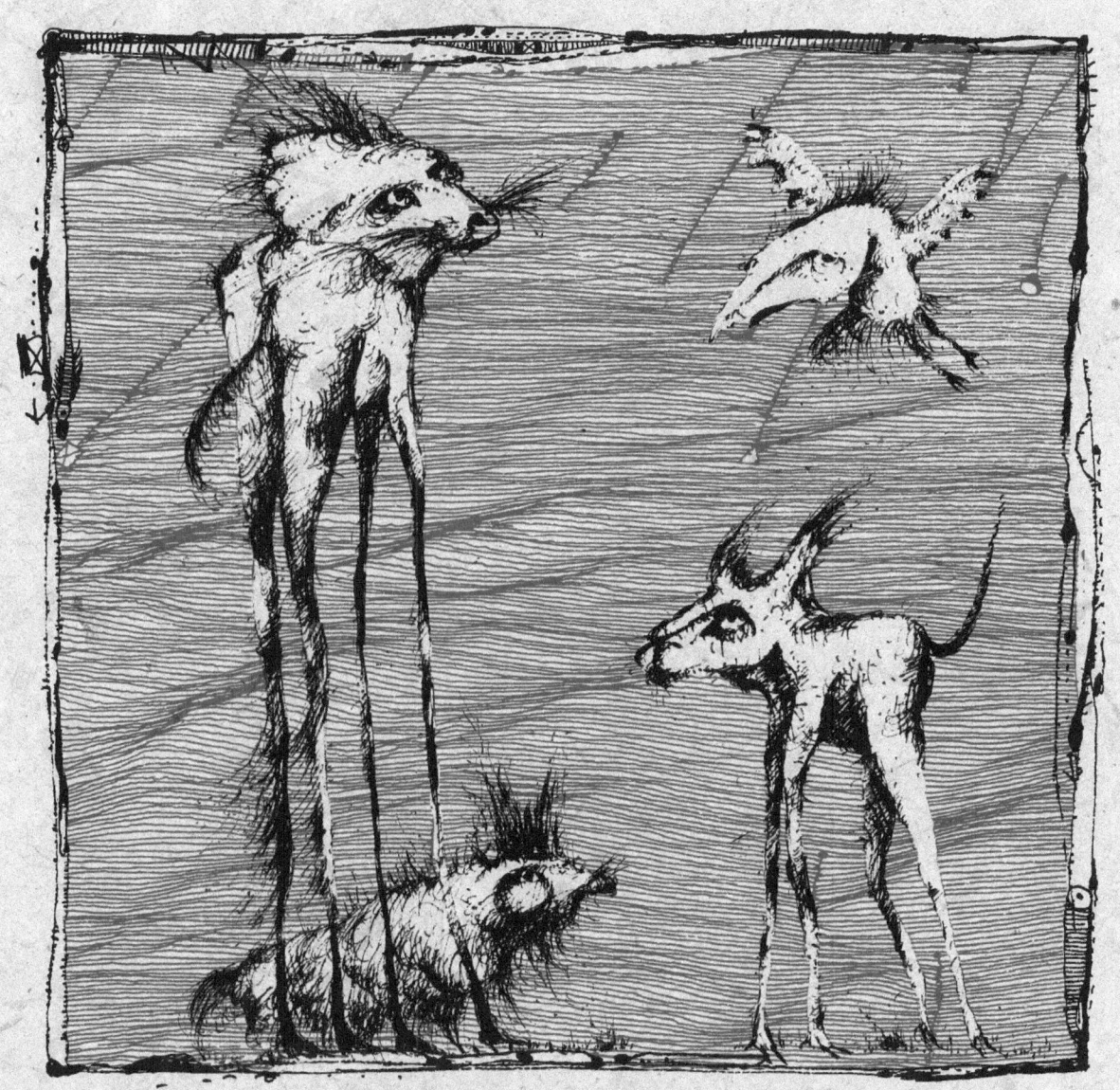

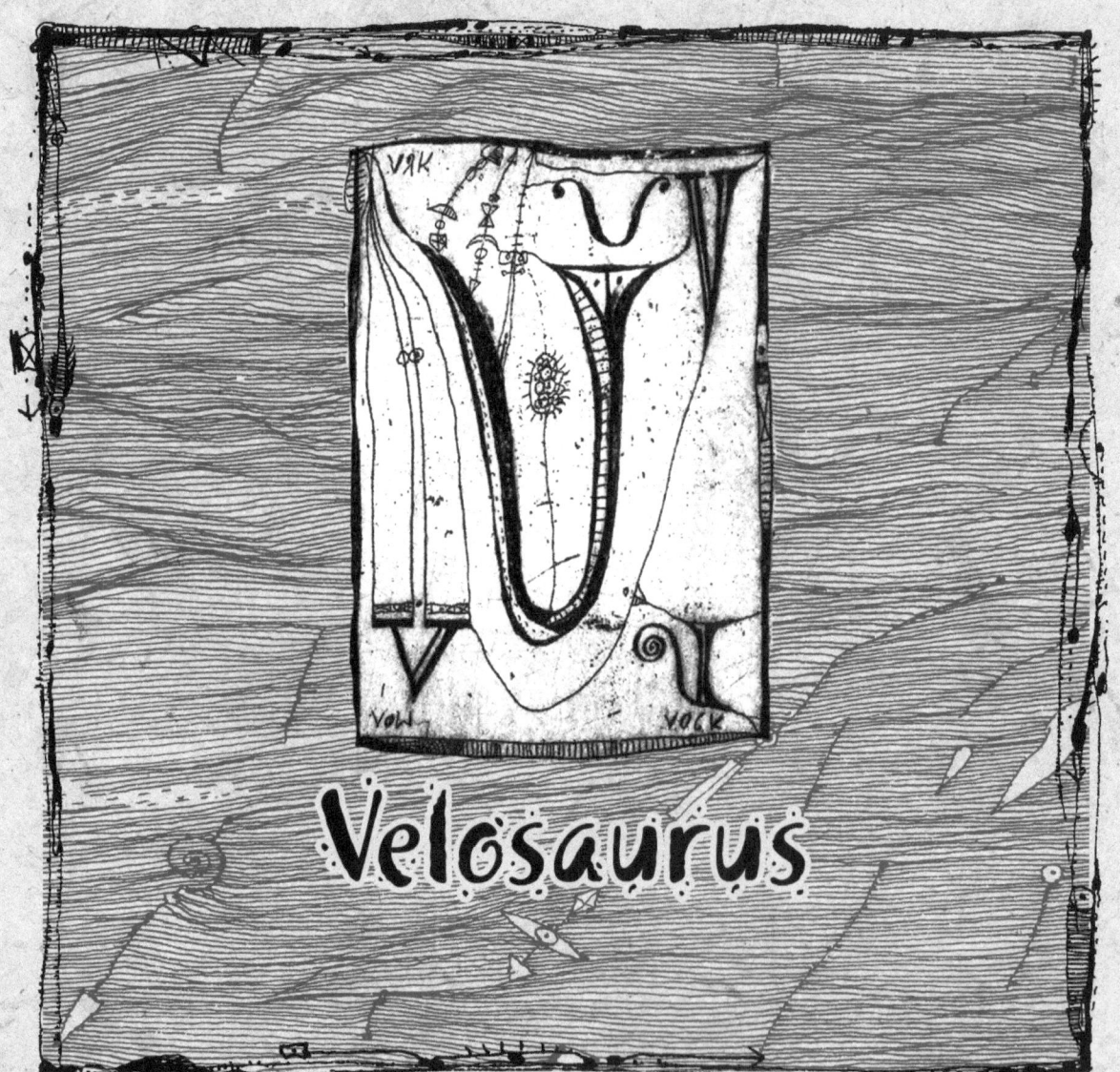

Velosaurus

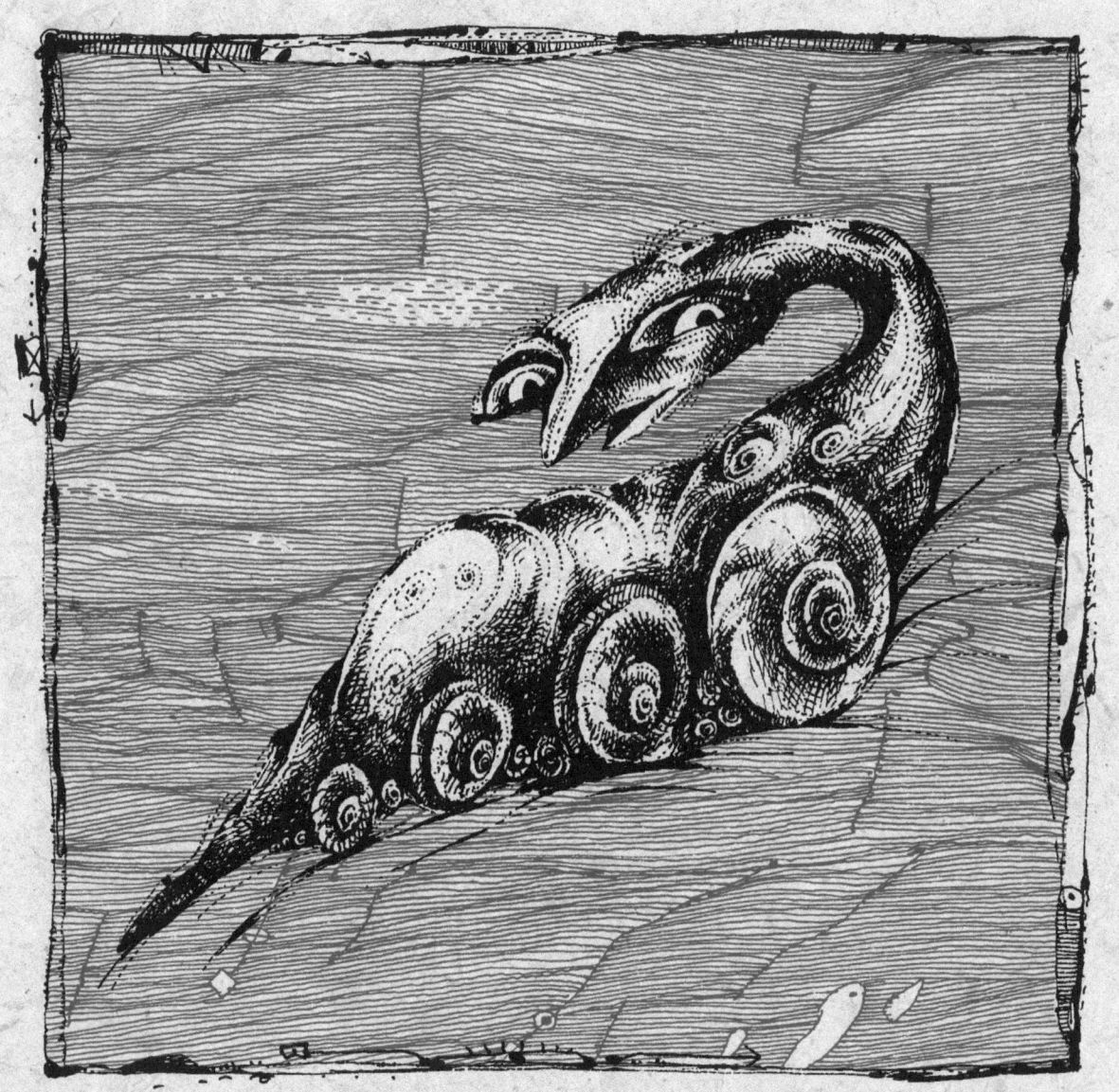

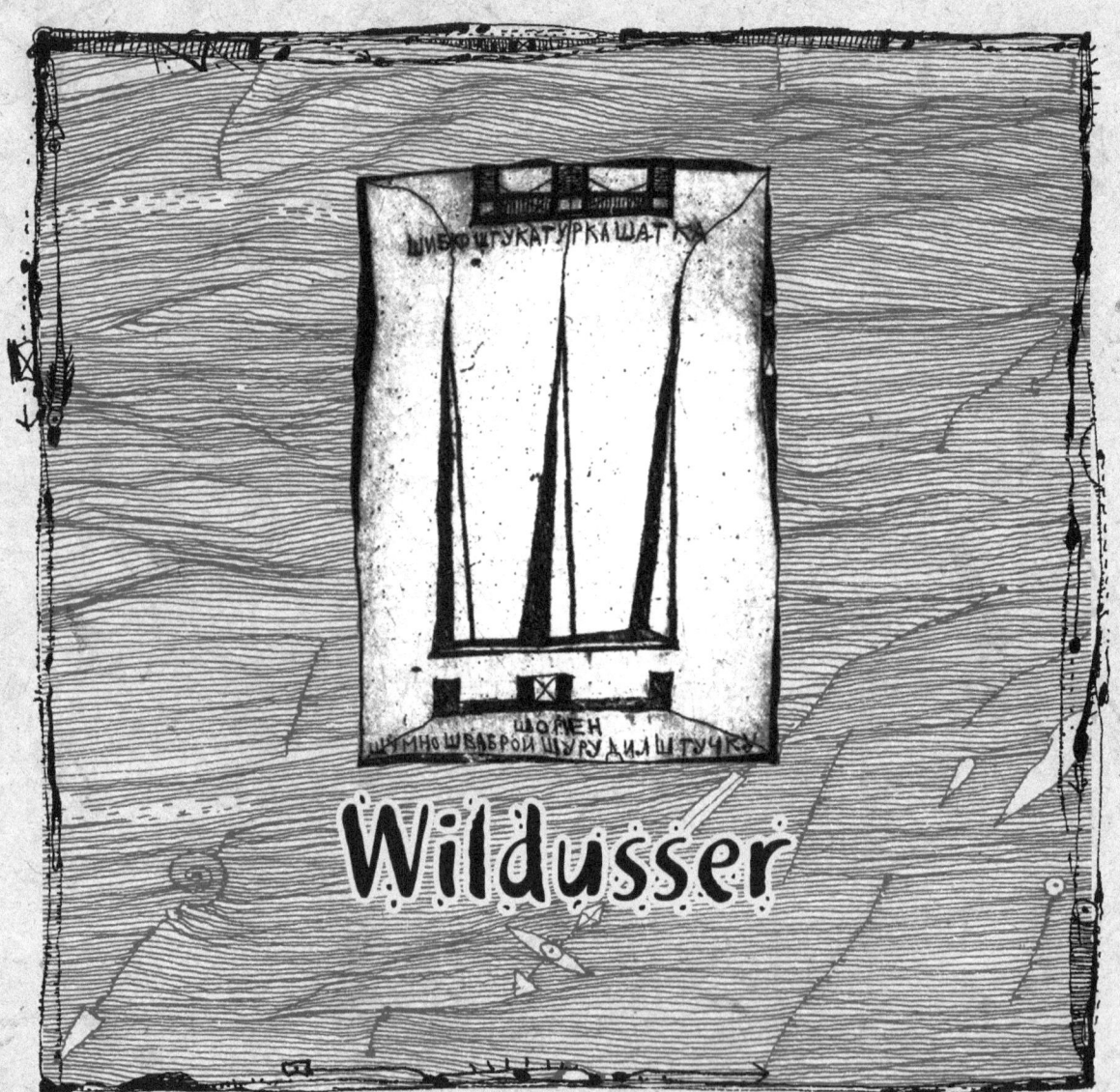

Wildusser

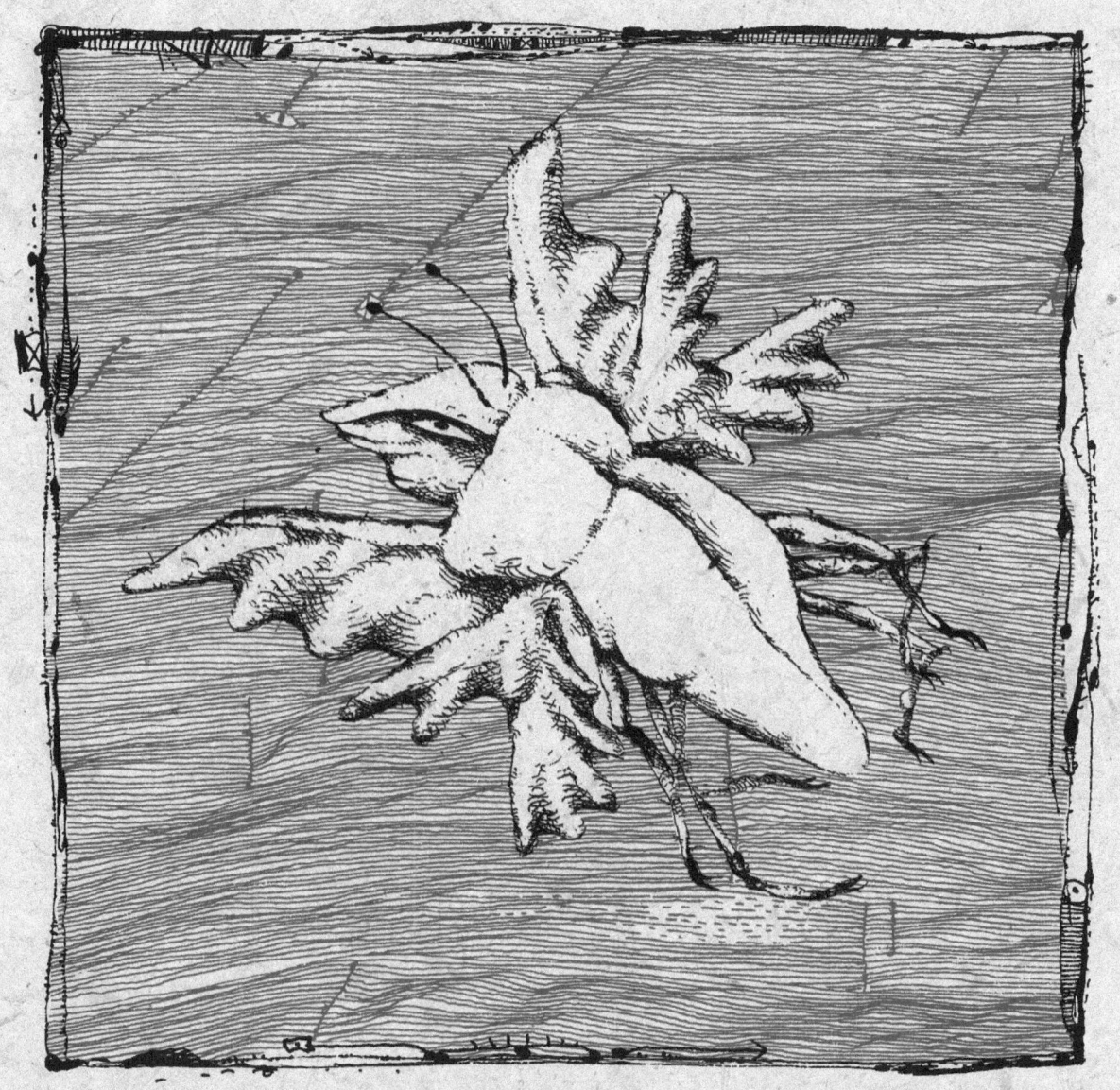

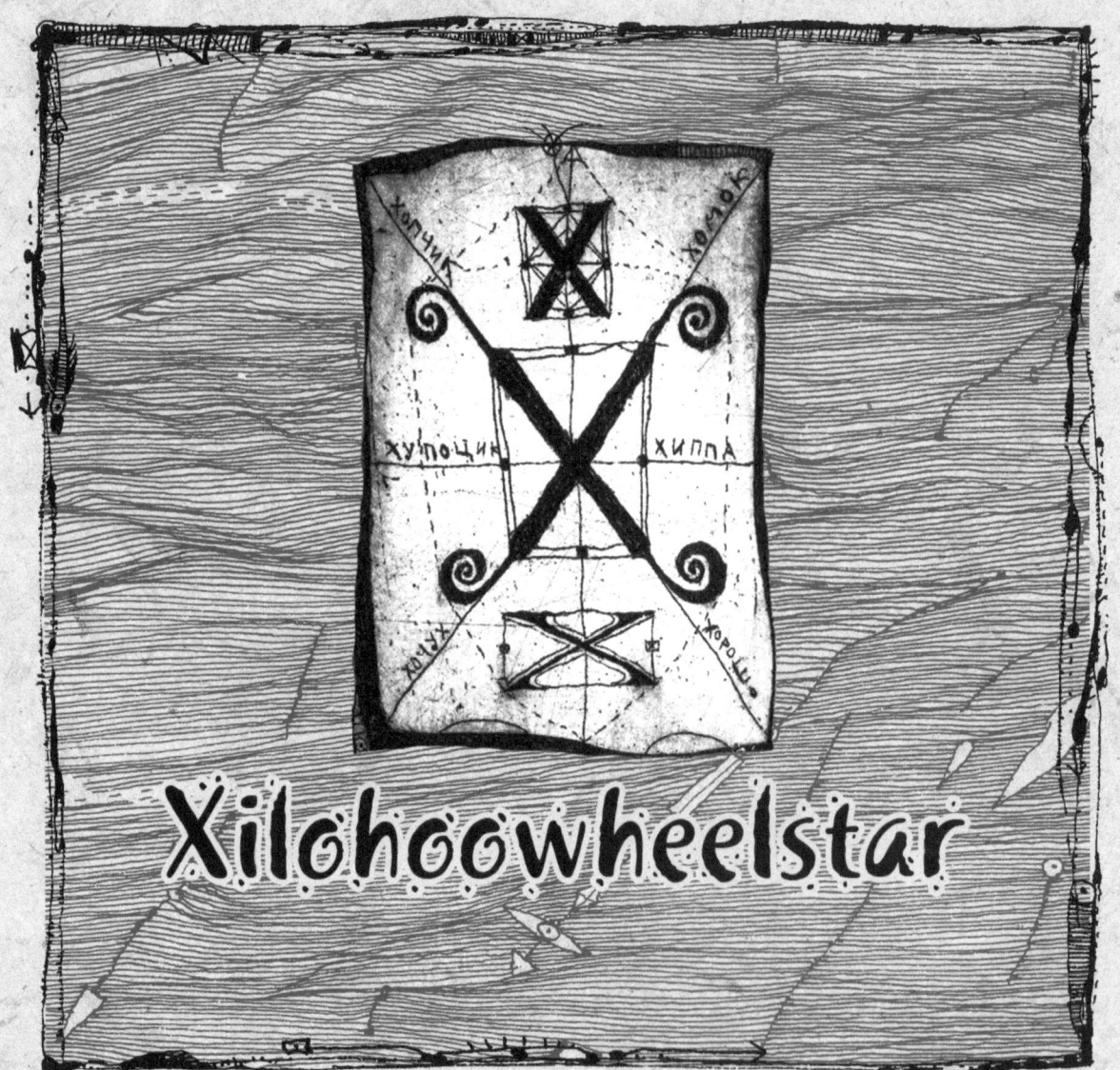

Xilohoowheelstar

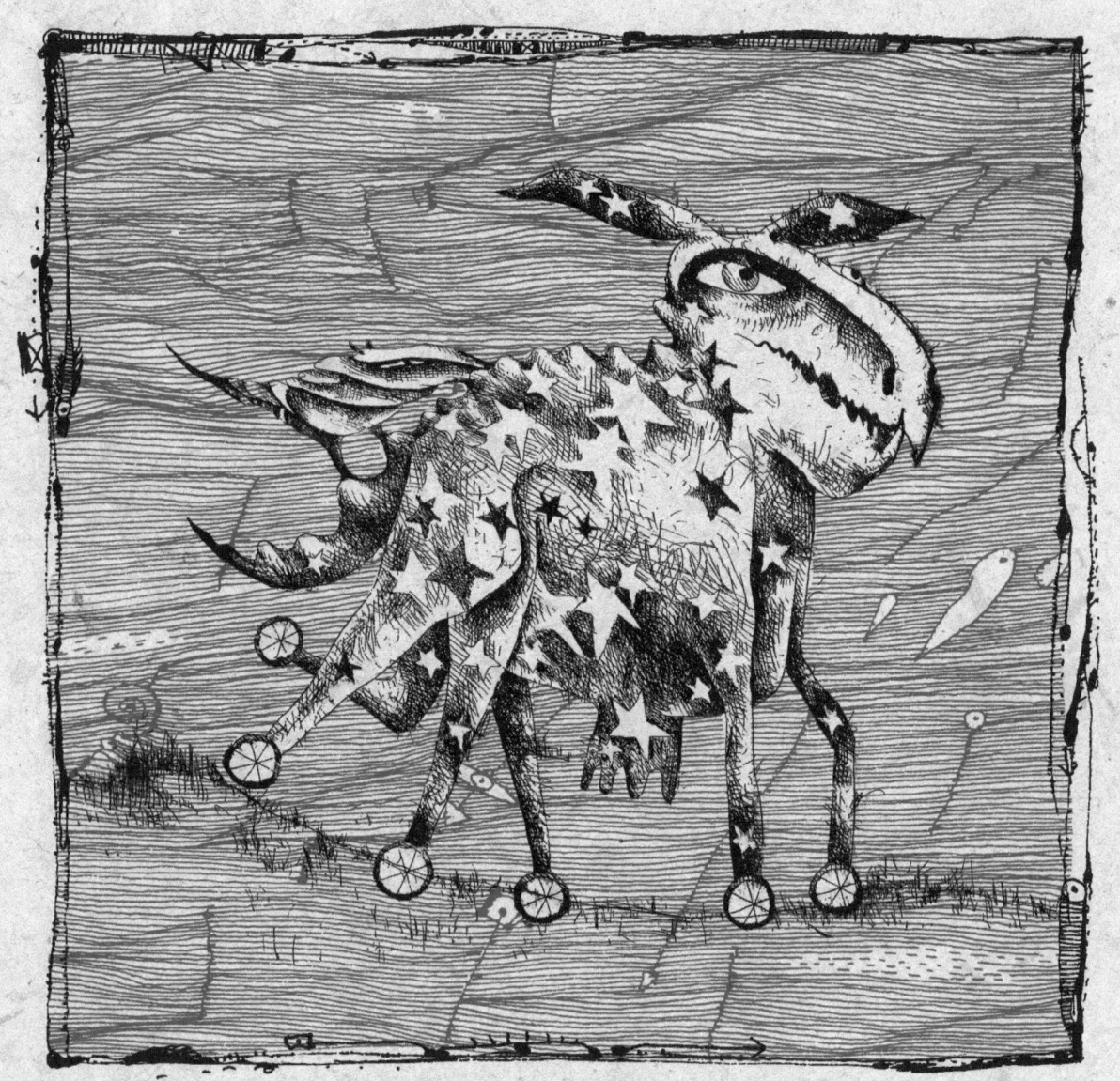

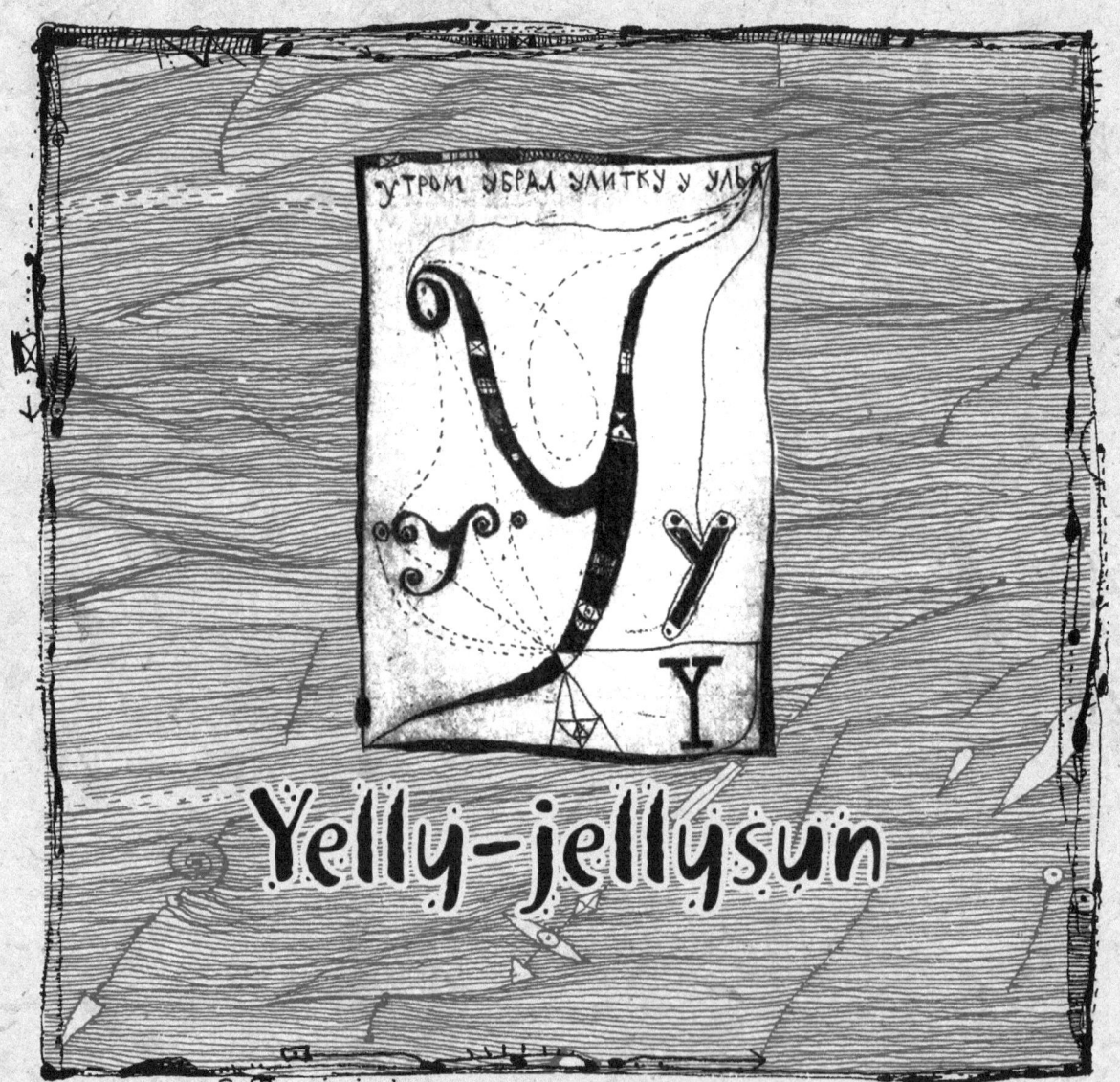

Утром убрал улитку у Ульи

Yelly-jellysun

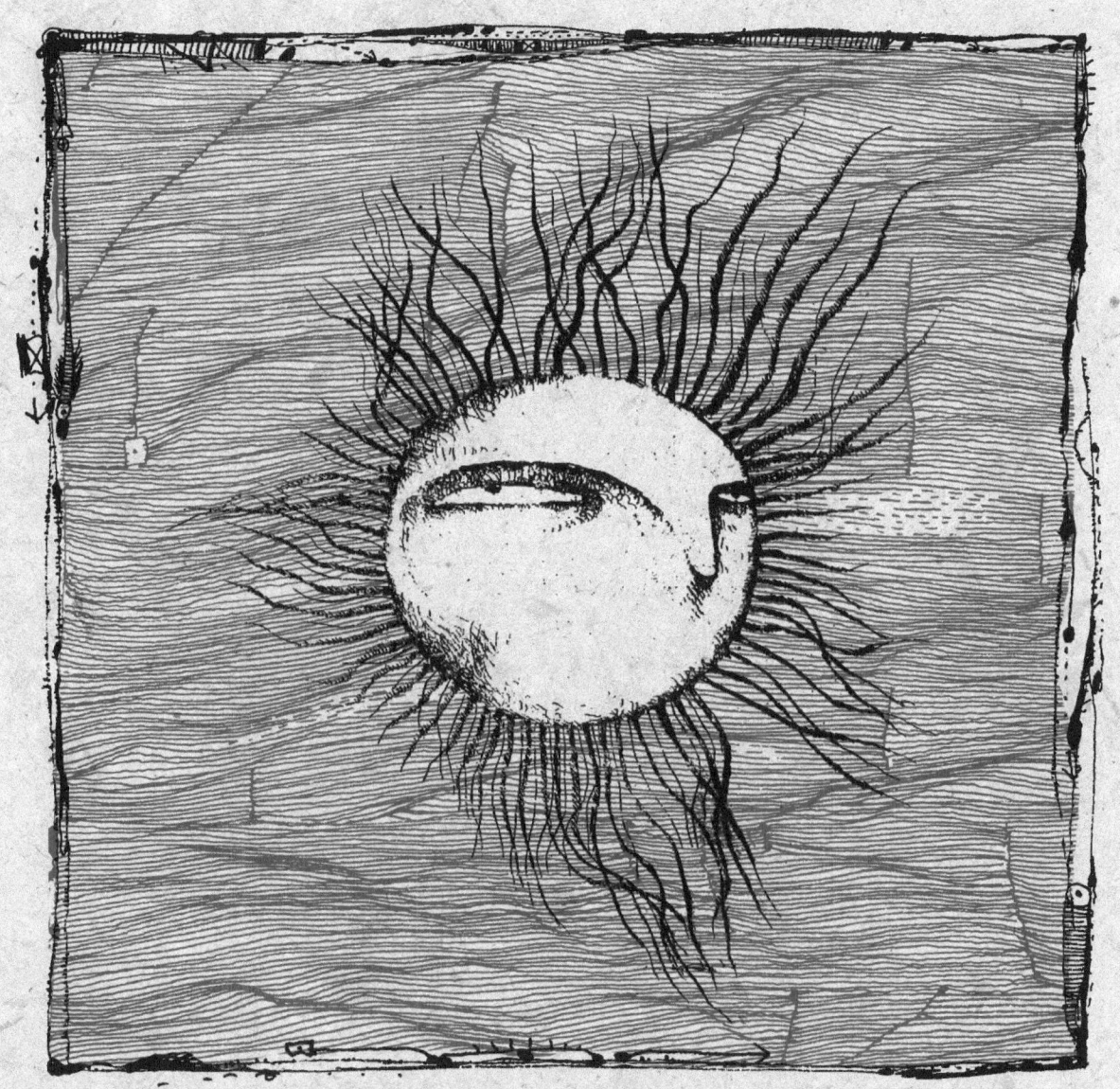

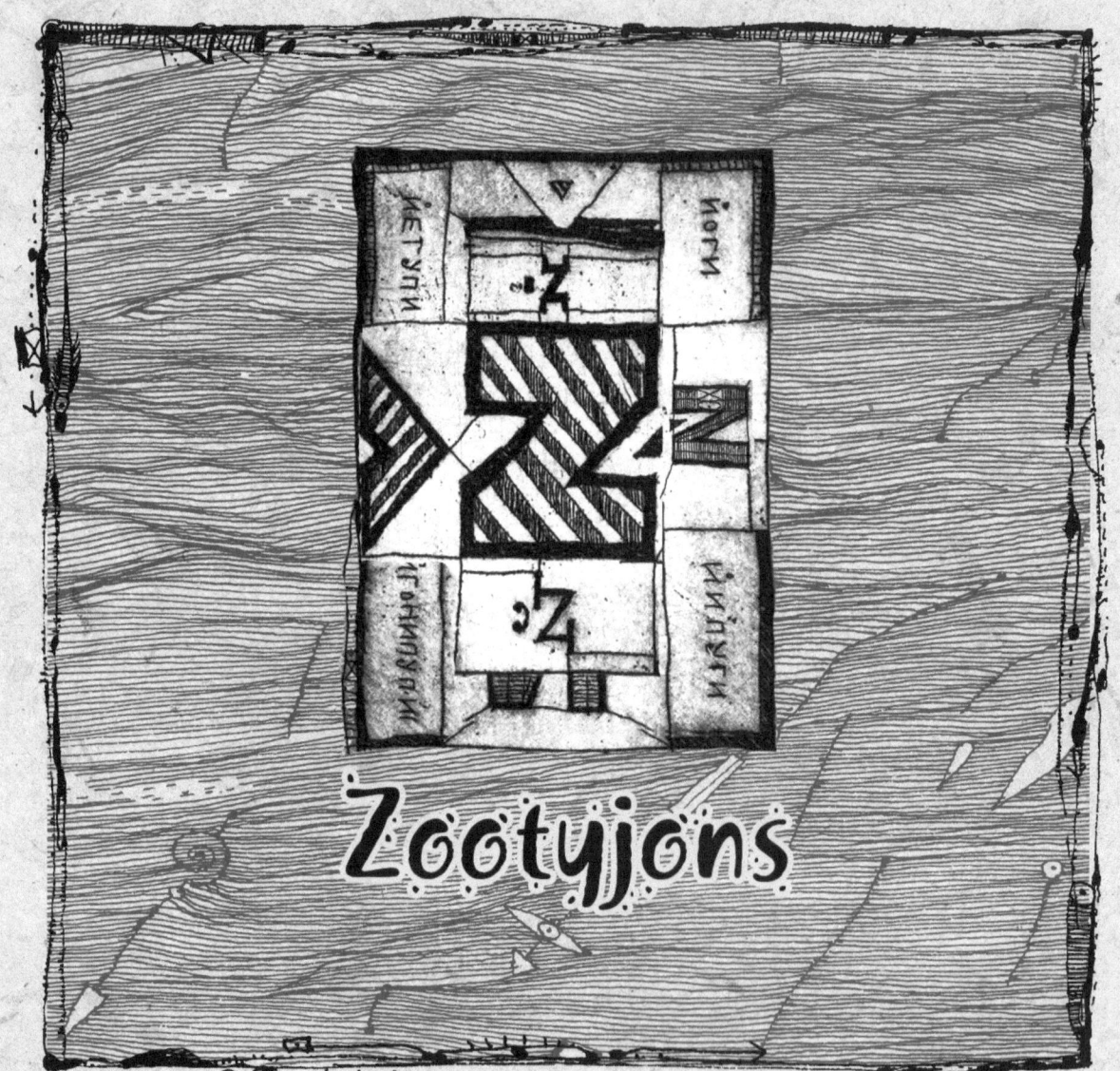

Zootyjons

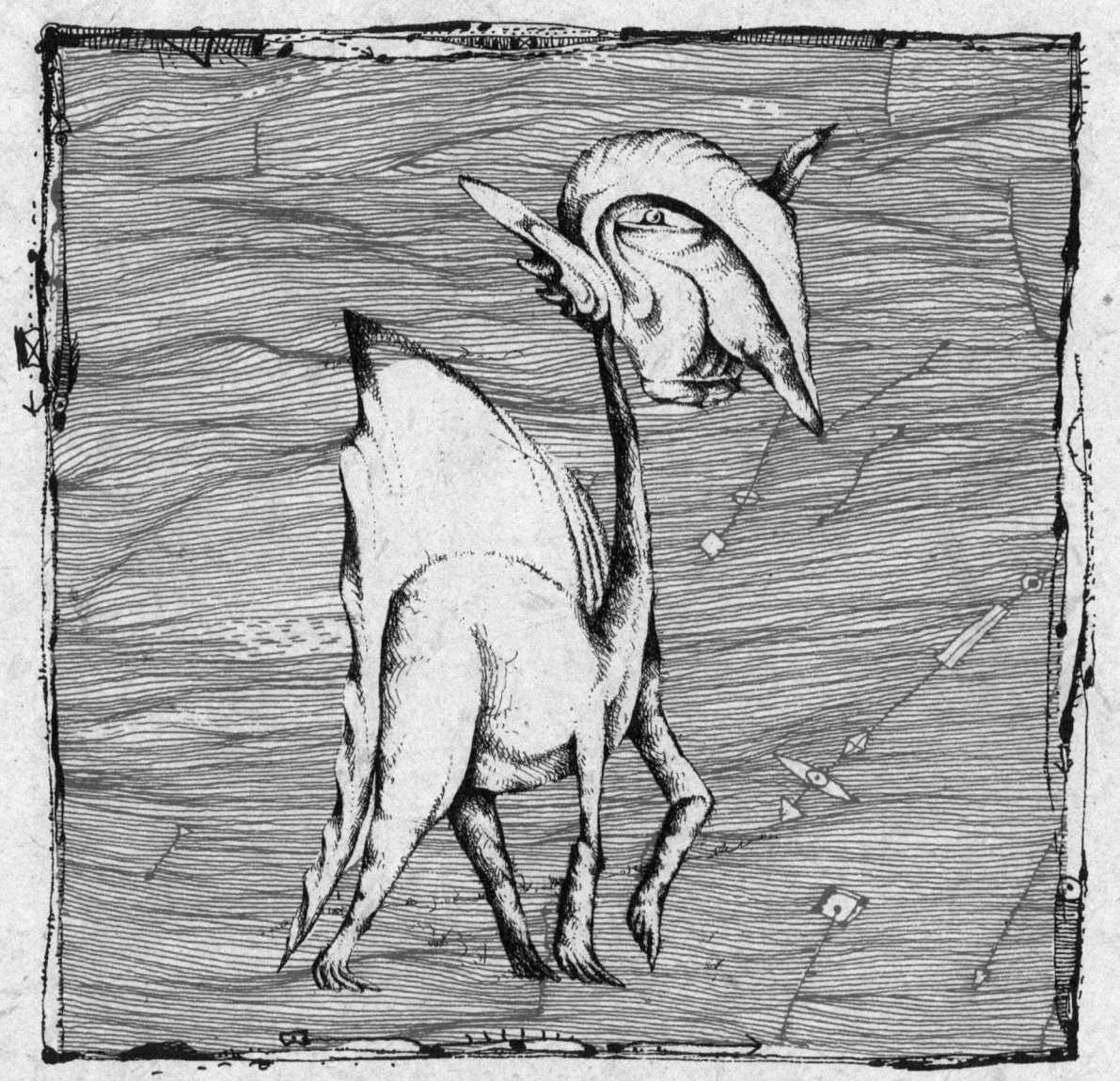

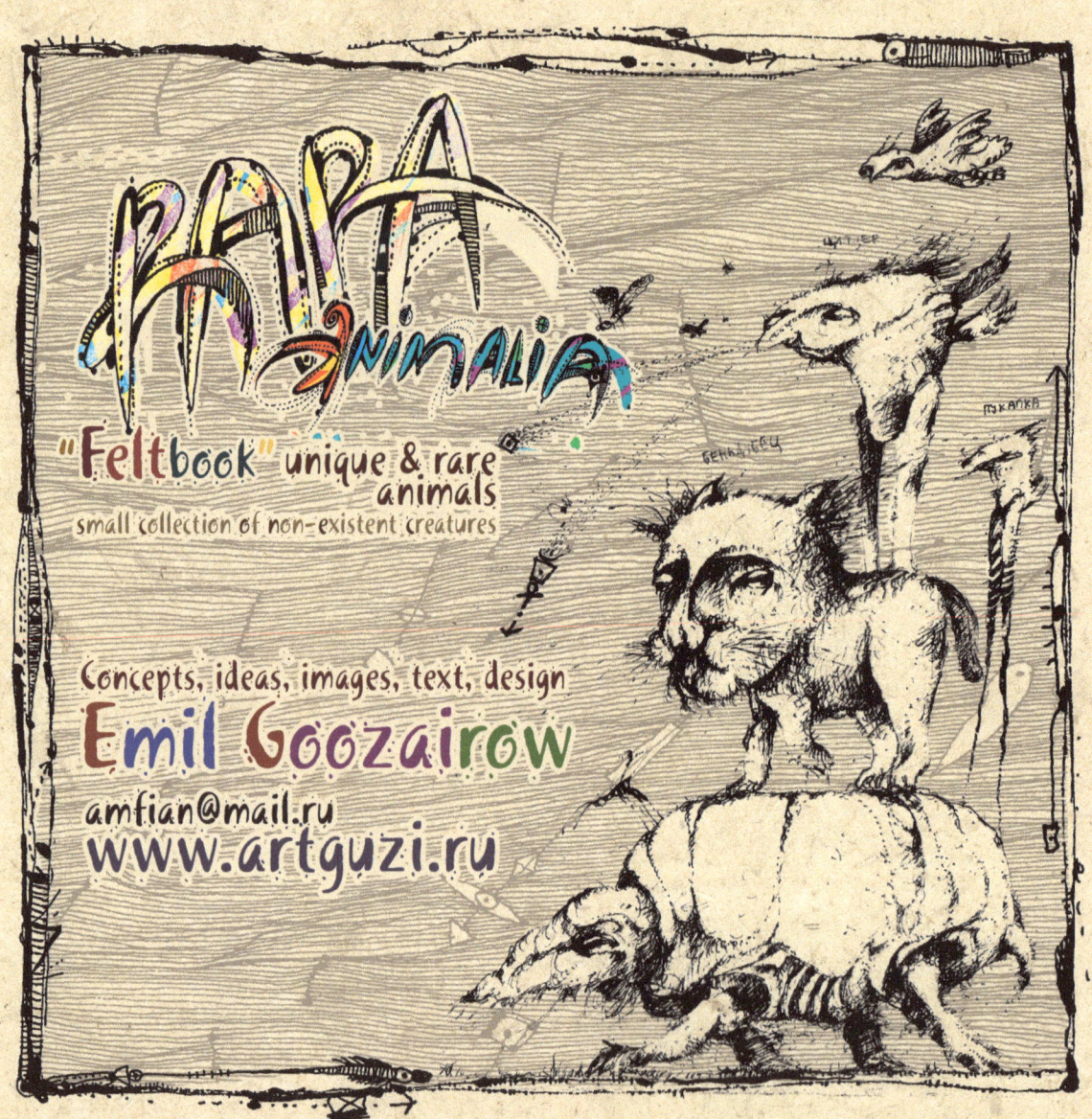

RARA animalia

"Feltbook" unique & rare animals
small collection of non-existent creatures

Concepts, ideas, images, text, design
Emil Goozairow
amfian@mail.ru
www.artguzi.ru